Teaching in Alaska: What I Learned in the Bush

Julie Bolkan

To Connie

For sweet friend
I always wished was
my neighbor!

Julie Bolkan

GladEye
Press

Springfield, Oregon

Teaching in Alaska: What I Learned in the Bush

Publisher and founder: Sharleen Nelson
Publisher and founder: J.V. Bolkan
Cover/Book Design and Production: J.V. Bolkan
Proofreaders: Sharleen Nelson, Melinda Pfrimmer, J.V. Bolkan

First Edition
Trade paperback ISBN: 978-0-9911931-7-2

Body text for this book is set in Garamond 12 pt. an old-style serif font based on the work of french designer Claude Garamond. It was chosen for its elegant, yet traditional feel and exceptional readability.

GladEye Press
Springfield, Oregon
www.gladeyepress.com

Dedication

To Bob Bolkan, the love of my life, who took me on this incredible journey.

Acknowledgments: Special thanks to my children, (Jeff, Mindy, Jason, and Aaron) and my extended family and friends, who without their love and support, I wouldn't have survived the first year.

Thanks also to the teaching staff, Carlton and Lucy Kuhns, Jerry and Helen Keller, Bill and Debbie Chalmers, Kathy Brown, Mindy and Tom McLaughlin, Suzanne Flemming, Ray and Marilyn, Peggy and Ken Groves, Robert and Billie Day, Cliff, Terry, Diana, Olinka, and Jim for your friendship and being our "family away from home".

I owe a debt of gratitude to the citizens of Akiak, Atmoutluk, and Quinhagak for their warm hospitality and for teaching me their customs and way of life.

Most of all, I want to express my appreciation to the students who warmed my heart with their innocence and excitement for learning.

Quyana! (Yup'ik for good luck) You all made my adventures in Bush Alaska special.

About the Author

 Julie Bolkan (Weninger) was born in North Dakota. Her family moved to the outskirts of Oregon City when she was a young child. Julie graduated from Oregon City High and married her childhood sweetheart Robert Bolkan. Together they raised their four children, Jeff, Mindy, Jason, and Aaron. Prior to her adventures in Alaska, she worked at Skipworth Juvenile Detention Center and for the Lane County (Eugene, Oreon) government. She and her husband spent approximately 12 years teaching and living in the remote Alaskan bush.

She resides in Springfield, Oregon with her two cats and is active in her church and keeping track of her growing collection of grandchilden (10) and great grandchildren (5).

Foreword

My parents, Bob and Julie Bolkan, started their journey to Akiak, Alaska on August 10,1980, the day after my wedding to Tom Mc-Laughlin. Nobody could have guessed that two years later, Tom and I, along with our 15 month-old-son, Brendan, would be joining them. It still amazes me that the timing of events allowed Tom the opportunity to accept his first teaching position in the same remote Eskimo village that my parents were teaching in. I am convinced that it was the power of my mother's prayers and desperate wishes that made it happen.

Living in the Alaskan Bush is not for the faint of heart. This was Dad's dream, not Mom's, but her love for him gave her the strength to at least try. They were midlife folks leaving a comfortable well-established life with a home, family, friends careers . . . all the things that they had spent nearly a quarter of a century building together. Yes, most of these things would still be there when they returned, but flying away from the familiar into so many unknowns was not an easy thing to do.

The culture shock, isolation, distance from family, and the incredibly harsh weather made their first two years in Akiak especially difficult for Mom. It would take a real sense of adventure and humor, an open mind, and a whole lot of creativity and ingenuity to make it work. They did make it work while building lifelong friendships and collecting memories of a lifestyle and culture that most people will never get to experience. The Yup'ik Eskimo people were very gracious in accepting us *gussacks* and welcoming us into their daily lives as well as teaching us and allowing us to participate in their culture.

Being in Akiak was a simpler lifestyle but that is not to be confused with boring or easy. It was similar to a pioneer life. We spent quality time with people we loved, or grew to love, less the distractions or conveniences of things such as phones, television, computers, stores, cars, indoor plumbing, etc. We truly felt the benefits from all the experiences, trials, and tribulations my parents went through prior to our arrival. They also created a very fun close-knit social circle with the other teachers that we were instantly inducted into. I am so grateful to have that opportunity to know my parents as "good friends".

When we left Akiak for the last time in 1985, Brendan had just turned four and our second son, Treg, was only nine months old. Our blue-eyed toeheaded boys were very popular with the village people but nobody was a bigger fan than their Grandma Julie. Mom and Brendan spent a lot of time together and shared a very special bond during our time in Akiak. Although my boys were too young to hold any real memories of their time in the village, I am so proud that they can claim it as part of their history.

The three years that I spent in Akiak is one of the most treasured segments of my life. I know that my dad loved Alaska from the very beginning and Mom grew to love it too. We all continued to live in different areas of Alaska for several years. Mom has been through experiences much more challenging than her time in Alaska and she continues to amaze me with her strength and determination. This is her story about her Alaskan Adventure. *Quyana* Mom for being the trailblazer on my adventures!

Mindy Pfrimmer

Jacksonville, Oregon

Year One: Akiak

Part dread. Part anticipation—my anxiety stemmed from uncertainty about what awaited us in Akiak, Alaska, a small village located on the west bank of the Kuskokwim River, 42 miles northeast of Bethel, on the Yukon–Kuskokwim Delta, where my husband Bob would be teaching for the next nine months, but mostly, it was flying for the first time in a small bush plane. This would be nothing like flying in a large commercial airplane with certified pilots.

After loading our luggage, which had to be distributed evenly so the plane wasn't too heavy on one side, we were crammed into small

seats like sardines in a can for the 30-mile, white-knuckle plane trip to the village.

Despite how much my husband Bob and Carlton Kuhns, the principal of the school who had come out to

A typical neighborhood view of Akiak, Alaska.

escort us from Bethel to Akiak, tried to distract me by pointing out scenery from the bush plane's small, dirt-smeared window, every tip of the wing made my heart beat faster.

Brown and desolate. As I gazed down from the air, it all looked the same. August is this region of Alaska's rainy season, so the river was high and muddy, resembling chocolate. The tundra was flat and brushy. We hadn't even arrived and already I felt a twinge of homesickness for the beautiful mountains overlooking our green Willamette valley; the tall majestic trees and clear running rivers and waterfalls of Oregon that we had left behind.

The plane finally touched down with a bumpy jolt on Akiak's uneven runway which was merely a clearing that resembled a cow pasture surrounded by small scrub trees. We carried our luggage down a muddy path about a quarter of a mile to the school. This would be our home for the school year. Carlton showed us the school where we found the boxes we had mailed earlier, and then he took us on a short tour of the village.

Carlton Kuhns

I had imagined neat little houses, but what I saw instead were small shacks, cabins, and a few that resembled tar paper houses. Scattered around the village among the tall grass and brush were discarded snowmobiles (the locals call them snow machines), old car and boat parts, and unwanted appliances that no longer worked. Chained along the riverbank and close to most of the buildings were scrawny, sad, blue-eyed sled dogs. Odors of drying fish hanging on racks, wet dogs, and open honey bucket holes permeated the air.

The name *Akiak* means "the other side," because it was a crossing to the Yukon River basin during the winter for area Yup'ik Eskimos. This place certainly felt about as far on "the other side" of the world as one could possibly get. How could Bob and I survive in this isolated place without our family and friends? Turning around and going home was not an option. "Don't worry Julie," Bob said. "It'll be fun. You'll see, it'll be just like a nine-month camping trip!"

The thought of a nine-month camping trip did not sound like a holiday. Because I had married a man who'd been raised in the outdoors, we did a lot of camping. Camping in the 60s and early 70s was still a primitive pastime that required a fair amount of work, especially with four children. When the kids were small we all slept in a tent. Later, the kids and the dog slept in the tent and Bobby and I slept in the station wagon. We had a fussy Coleman gas lantern and a camp stove, but mostly we cooked over the campfire.

Bob loved camping and fishing, as did the kids. I, on the other hand, found it more work than fun. After the kids were in school and I was working part time doing clerical work, getting ready and packing the food and gear took me a good part of the week. Being the queen of worry, I was constantly counting heads to be sure my four kids were safe while at the camp, and then coming home tired and having to unpack and clean up everything seemed to take the rest of the week. The thing about camping is that you mostly do it in the summer when the weather is pretty dependable, you do it for a relatively short amount of time, and you're really never more than a day away from 'civilization" if an emergency arises, or if you just run out of hot chocolate. A makeshift forest outhouse may not be pleasant, but knowing that your porcelain toilet awaits at the end of the weekend, or even week-long trip makes it easier to deal with it.

Our History

Twenty three years earlier my fairy tale dream had been to simply marry my high school sweetheart, Bobby Bolkan, have a houseful of babies, a few cats, and live happily ever after in comfortable suburbia.

We grew up together in the small Oregon town of Redland, an unincorporated community located in Clackamas County six miles east of Oregon City and four miles south of Carver. The community was named for the color of the soil there. Remarkably, both of our families migrated to Oregon from North Dakota at about the same time in the 1930s.

My father Moritz Weninger was born in Russia to German parents who emigrated to the United States and settled in North Dakota when he was five-years old. The Weningers were farmers and Moritz grew up with his nine brothers and sisters working the farmland. In 1933, he married my mother Odelia Weigel. She was the oldest daughter of a family of 14 children who lived on a neighboring farm.

Moritz and Odelia started their own farm, and over the next three years welcomed two daughters to their family—my older sister Tillie and me. In 1937, after two years of crop failures, they sold their farm at auction and bought train tickets to move their family to Oregon, where most of my mother's family had already settled.

Starting their life in Oregon was hard; living with relatives until they could afford a place of their own. My dad worked for other farmers and rented a one-room cabin without running water or electricity. Mom carried water from a spring, cooked on a wood stove, and we had a chamber pot under the bed. We had a cow and planted a large garden. Our family increased when my two brothers were born, Willy in 1939 and Johnny in 1940. By this time my dad was hired to manage a small dairy and fruit orchard. We had a two-bedroom house with running water and electricity.

When I was eight-years old my father got a job in the paper mill in Oregon City and moved the family to Redland onto a 10-acre parcel that had a small house that had once served as a gas station with living quarters in the back. We finally had a place of their own. Dad had an income and could now be a gentleman farmer. We had electricity, but no indoor plumbing. There was a well outside with a hand pump and a path to the outhouse. We attended a one-room school house that was within walking distance. In 1948, my sister Rosella was born, and three years later, my youngest sister Patty.

Bobby also grew up in the rural area outside of Oregon City. Although the two North Dakota families did not know each other in 1937, the Bolkan family, (Gustavas and Mary Ethel Bolkan) packed their belongings and eight of their 11 children into a used hearse that they referred to as the "popcorn wagon" to keep from frightening the children, and drove to Oregon, the land of plenty. Bob was 18 months old when he arrived. His large family were loggers, making a living off the old-growth timber in the area.

Bobby grew up to be a strong young man of Norwegian heritage who'd been raised with hard physical work in the woods and in their small, family-operated sawmill. He was also smart enough, and ambitious enough, to go to college so that he wouldn't have to be a logger the rest of his life.

In the fall of 1957, Bob and I were married. Our first child Jeff arrived in the fall of 1958, followed by his sister Mindy in 1959. By 1960, Bob had graduated from Portland State College and he took a position as the teacher at Skipworth Juvenile Detention Center in Eugene, Oregon. Over the next few years, we rounded out our family with two more boys, Jason and Aaron.

Through the 60s, we lived the stereotypical suburban family life. Bob was a gifted teacher, able to relate to even the most challenging students in the juvenile delinquent system. A physically imposing, well-muscled 6'3" man with a bushy, mountain man beard, he was a gentle teacher with a fully developed sense of humor and a seemingly endless well of empathy for the kids caught up in the system.

Getting away with the family into the outdoors was Bob's way of recharging and being able to work with the kids who needed so much from him. Eventually, however, it became too much, and in 1978, after 18 years teaching delinquent kids, he was completely burnt out. He withdrew his retirement, bought a commercial fishing boat and tried his hand at salmon fishing on the Oregon coast.

Like many of his ventures, fishing was not as profitable as he had hoped. To support his family he ended up doing a variety of jobs. Because he came from a large family of loggers he gravitated toward working with wood. He made beautiful myrtle wood bowls, vases, and some furniture. Some he sold at bazaars and gift shops, but most were given away. He cut cord wood, bought and logged cedar sales, and made cedar shakes (shingles).

Until one day he saw an ad at the University of Oregon for teachers in Alaska. Bob had always been fascinated by the idea of Alaska. Teaching in Alaska was a dream opportunity for him. In the late 60s he had applied to teach in American Samoa. It was so exciting.

We had numerous meetings and saw a video of the island. Bob was accepted to teach, but he would have to go without his family. The housing was limited and could not accommodate a family with children, so Bob declined the position.

But now, with all of our kids finished with high school, with the exception of our youngest, who was to be a senior the next year, I no longer had the excuse that uprooting my small children and taking them to a harsh environment was impractical. Plus, he promised our next adventure would be a warm, tropical island.

Stopover in Bethel

Bob was offered a position of teaching math and science at a high school in Akiak, Alaska starting in August 1980. Before the Molly Hooch Act was passed in 1974, the villages in Alaska had Bureau of Indian Affair schools for elementary school children, grades 1–8. There were no high schools in most Alaskan villages. High School age children were sent to boarding schools either in Anchorage, Oklahoma, or Oregon. This was a disastrous policy—dropout rates for native high school students were as high as 65 percent. Worse, the policy of moving students out of their villages was seriously harming the native social structures. Tragically, the policies were harming the students the most—alcoholism, suicide, loss of cultural identity, and a host of related social problems were nearly endemic among the displaced teenagers.

The Molly Hooch Act (officially named Tobeluk v. Lind) specified that children should be able to attend high school in their home towns. Therefore, a State School and qualified teachers were to be made available in every village. By 1978, the State of Alaska had spent $140 million building and outfitting high schools throughout the vast Alaskan bush. All these new schools needed teachers.

In 1980, we were in our mid-40s and really hadn't spent much time at all outside of Oregon. We were over the moon excited to be flying to this far off land. I had flown only once before in a commercial airplane and I think it was Bob's first flight. I quit my job at Lane County Housing and Social Services. Because my monthly paycheck was mostly what we were living on, there wasn't anything left to save up for the airfare and one month's living expenses before our first Alaskan paycheck. So we began our Great Alaskan adventure in debt.

Our whole life was in turmoil as we prepared for the trip—getting a barge order of supplies shipped to our village, packing what we could take with us, and shipping boxes ahead. And if that wasn't enough to stress me out, our only daughter was getting married the Saturday before we left. We prepared all the food for the reception and decorated the hall. The wedding was at the Owen Rose Garden in Eugene and the reception at Marist High School.

Everything went well until we got home and looked at our plane tickets one last time to verify the time our flight left from Portland on Monday morning. Our tickets were dated for Sunday morning, not Monday as we had planned. Some of our friends and family were still visiting from the wedding. My friend Marilynn and our neighbors, Vic and Marilla stayed until 1:00 a.m. to help us. They were night owls and usually didn't go to bed until late anyway. Of course, they could sleep in the next morning. There wasn't time for Bob and me to sleep. We finished packing and doing last minute things to the house and left for the airport at 5:30 in the morning. Maybe we could sleep on the plane, we thought. Going into our sons' room at 5:00 a.m. to say goodbye seems like yesterday. I can still feel the horrible ache of leaving my children. I couldn't sleep on the plane and had to wear my sunglasses to cover my red eyes from crying most of the flight.

The first leg of our journey began with a four-hour flight from Oregon to Anchorage. Because it was Sunday, there wasn't a connecting flight to Bethel until the next morning—another change in our agenda and added expense. We had to spend the night in a hotel in Anchorage. This turned out to be a blessing in disguise, however. We ended up getting a good night's sleep before arriving in Bethel. The plane from Anchorage to Bethel was the size of the commuter planes that shuttle the 100-mile stretch between Eugene and Portland. They referred to it as a bush plane simply because it flew into the Alaskan bush.

We landed in the small, isolated town of Bethel, Alaska on a dreary August afternoon. Bethel is the hub for the Yukon Kuskokwim Delta and lies approximately 400 miles west of Anchorage. The population in 1980 was less than 4,000. Bethel has a seawater port that can receive shipments by barge when the river is not frozen. This barge also delivered to the villages along the Kuskokwim River usually until October or until the river started to freeze. This was the barge that was scheduled to bring our winter supplies of food to the village. The only other transportation to Bethel was by bush plane.

Parts of Alaska are known for large mosquitoes, but those we encountered in Bethel could qualify as the Alaskan state bird. Besides mosquitoes there were other annoying bugs referred to as "no-see-ums." They were tiny insects with a mighty sting. Outside in a yard I saw a small child with black specks on his face. Wondering if the child was ill or had some strange affliction, my curiosity was aroused. I discovered that the child's mother had rubbed Crisco on his face and exposed skin. I soon learned that Crisco had many uses in the bush. Generously slathered onto the skin, the slippery stuff trapped the mosquitoes or no-see-ums and prevented them from stinging. They could be brushed off later.

A van picked us up at the airport and took us and our meager belongings to Bethel's high school where we met other teachers and principals. We would be spending several days in an orientation session to become familiar with village life and customs. Our host family housed us during our stay. I don't remember the host family's name, but they were very kind and supplied us with fresh fruit and vegetables at every meal. I didn't understand how generous and special that was until later when I was unable to have an apple or fresh carrot. There would be no fresh fruit, vegetables, or dairy products in the village.

After a few weeks the craving gets acute. I realized that I had taken food, that essential of life, for granted. After returning to work once the children were all in school, I easily slipped into buying all the time-saving benefits of the foods available from the local supermarkets. I still baked bread when I found time, but it was so much easier to buy a loaf already sliced. I could get tomatoes, lettuce, and virtually any fruit I wanted, fresh—yearround. In Akiak, these food items would become a luxury and only available on a trip to Bethel.

A round-trip flight on a bush plane from the village to Bethel for me would be $80, plus the cost of fruit and veggies. Not only was produce way too expensive, it wasn't even good quality.

During our stay in Bethel, our hosts took us on a tour of the city, the bank where we opened a checking account, the two grocery/hardware stores where we could get needed supplies until our barge order arrived, the Bureau of Indian Affairs Hospital, Family Clinic, the Bethel Hotel, and "McSwanson," the only fast food restaurant in town at that time.

Bethel was the main airport for flights to all the Lower Kuskokwim villages. Planes landing and taking off from Bethel were only allowed to carry a limited amount of weight. In addition to weighing your luggage, each traveler was asked to step on the scale. Some families had cars or pickups brought in by barge even though there were fewer than 20 miles of road in the entire city. ATVs, snow machines, and taxis were the main mode of transportation. Because the taxis charged by the individual there was a flat rate charge per person. Sometimes a ride from the airport entailed dropping off three or four people before you reached your destination. They usually waited until they had a full cab.

I found Bethel to be desolate and foreign to anything I was used to. There were no pretty yards with flowers, no beautiful trees, only tall dry grass, tied-up barking dogs, discarded appliances, and junk that lined the yards. There was an unfamiliar smell of dry fish and some smell I couldn't identify. The buildings were insulated with yellow foam that had been blown on the outside, which made them look like something from a science fiction movie. If I was this disappointed with Bethel, I wondered what lay in store for us in Akiak where we were going to live and teach.

The small village of Akiak, with a population of about 200 people, is approximately 30 miles from Bethel. The plane we were going to take from Bethel to the village was the size of a private plane with seating room for four people, including the pilot. The principal for our school was Carlton Kuhns. Carlton grew up in the Midwest and was a delightful young man not much older than my sons. Carlton had a huge smile and a warm heart as big as Alaska. I had heard so much about the bush planes and how dangerous they were. I was terrified of flying in one but because it was the only option for getting to the village I had to do it.

Carlton made the short trip almost enjoyable with his constant reassurance that everything would be just fine. What were these people like? Do they even want us in their small village? Nothing could have prepared Bob and me, (a couple of tall *gussocks*, which in Yup'ik is a less than endearing term for white people) for the culture shock that awaited us.

Even though Carlton had tried to prepare us for what we'd find in Akiak, my first views as we flew in were dismay and more than a little confusion.

Akiak Infrastructure

You don't think that much about how roads define the look of a town or city, until you arrive at a place without them. Because there were no cars in Akiak, there was no need for roads. Paths leading to buildings, down to the river, and to the airstrip were all they needed. The permafrost was about six feet deep so the top layer of soil was not as unstable as the tundra villages and they didn't need boardwalks. Although there was a boardwalk around the school.

Another view of housing in Akiak.

Almost everyone had three wheelers, snow machines, and boats. At one time small wooden cabins had lined the Kuskokwim River, but the river bank was constantly eroding which caused many of the houses to be rebuilt further away from the river. The housing consisted of mostly little cabins situated randomly around the village.

The Alaska Native Claims Settlement Act was signed into law by President Richard M. Nixon on December 18, 1971, the largest land claims settlement in US history. The settlement established Alaska Native claims to the land by transferring titles to more than 200 local village corporations. The corporations were the governing bodies of the villages, much like the county and city officials in most of the lower 48 states. Natives were entitled to apply for a parcel of land from the corporations.

Winters were extremely cold and small dwellings were more practical to heat. Because of the freezing winters, the only building that had heated plumbing (running water) was the new State School. To insulate and protect the pipes from freezing was a large undertaking and could not be afforded by the general population. Most residents carried water from the river and used honey buckets in their homes. A typical honey bucket was a five-gallon bucket sometimes with a toilet seat on top that was used as an indoor toilet. Outside each house was a hole dug down to the permafrost and covered with a board. This is where the honey bucket from inside the house was emptied.

As a child growing up during the Depression era of the 1930s I took it for granted that the bathroom was at the end of a path outside. I think my trouble with honey buckets started at an early age. Probably can't count the number of my sister's bracelets that were lost down that outhouse.

There was one two-seater outhouse by the old Bureau of Indian Affairs (BIA) school that was used while the BIA school was operating. It could only be used in warmer weather. I heard stories that you could literally freeze your butt off if you used it in the freezing weather. Although it wasn't yet winter, this particular outhouse was unusable because some residents had been using it as a dump for their honey buckets and the debris was overflowing.

An arctic food cache.

Honey buckets proved to be a large problem for me. One very cold windy morning I took the honey bucket out to empty it. As I picked up the bucket a gust of wind blew it all over me. At the time it wasn't funny, but now I can see some humor in it. Especially when I came back into the house and Bob's not-so-empathetic observation was, "You have shit freckles."

Most buildings had arctic porches and outside caches for food storage. Arctic porches were designed as entryways where you would go in and shut the door so the extreme cold air could not blow directly into your living space. Many people used this as a place to take off their boots and parkas. The cache was a food storage building built on stilts to keep wild animals out.

Each extended family had their own steam house. Other than a wash-tub in the kitchen, that was their only method of bathing. Beside the State school that housed grades 1–12 and the old BIA building, there was a Moravian Church, Ivan's "under-the-bed" store, a clinic, and a post office. The village had electric power supplied by a generator. Power was not the most reliable. We quickly learned to always have a flashlight, matches, and candles handy for when the generator would shut down.

A single party-line phone was shared by three villages. Good luck trying to make a call from that phone. If you did get an open line and connected with your party, it was a dollar a minute to talk. The school and many of the natives had CB radios to communicate with each other and nearby villages. There was also a daily announcement on the "Tundra Drums" radio program between 8:00 and 8:30 each morning and 4:30 to 5:00 each afternoon. Anyone could notify the Tundra Drums in Bethel and ask that their message be aired.

The first family we met in Akiak was the Williams', Tim, Helena, and their children. They were one of the three most influential families in the village. Their ancestors were some of the first who settled in Akiak years ago. Tim and Helena had lost a son from alcohol over-dose. Another son Gerald was married and lived in another village. They had three children living with them.

They had recently built a building to use as a small store, but were willing to rent it to teachers for $500 a month, until new teacher housing could be built. It consist-ed of one room and arctic porch. The building had only one door that didn't have a lock and two small windows. This lack of egress never would have passed inspec-tion for a rental or living situations in the lower 48. There was an oil

Bob in our first Akiak house.

heater in the middle of the room and a curtained area with a honey bucket that served as the bathroom. In one corner was a homemade bed about 18 inches off the floor. On the bare plywood frame was a four-inch piece of foam that served as our mattress. Needless to say, we were starting out on our nine-month camping trip without any frills.

A daybed in disrepair with an old throw to cover the wear was our only living room furniture. For our kitchen area we had a six-foot counter with a shelf underneath; no cupboard doors. A poorly made table with two benches served as our dining area. We had a two-burner hotplate to cook on, our ice chest was our refrigerator, and we used the arctic porch as our freezer. A huge garbage can held our water. Bob used two five-gallon buckets to carry water from the school to add to our water supply. Our garbage was either thrown into the honey-bucket hole unless it was flammable and could be taken to the school for burning.

The well water at the school was so rusty it looked like weak coffee and tasted horrible. After it sat for a while some of the rust settled and it was almost drinkable if we mixed it with tang or made coffee. It didn't take long for my hair to turn a rusty shade of brown.

After I saw the village and our living conditions, my heart sank even further. What had I gotten myself into? I was more than 3,000 miles away from my children and extended family. My son Jeff and his family were living in California; My daughter Mindy had gotten married the weekend before we left and was planning to live in our house with her husband and keep an eye on Aaron who was a senior at Marist; and Jason was attending Oregon State University. I was already missing them.

We had shipped ahead our eating utensils, plates, cups, pots and pans, dish pans, linens, pillow, warm quilts, a radio/tape player, a small TV, candles, and a coffee pot, but found out there was always something else we needed. Family and friends at home were wonderful. I would send them my lists and with their help we were able to make our living conditions almost cozy. I obtained material to make curtains for the cupboards and windows. We also hung bed sheets from a wire for a little more privacy in our sleeping quarters.

Privacy was important—we had to share the tiny space with another single teacher. There was no other option but to rent this building for the start of the school year. We consoled ourselves that at least it was only temporary until the teacher housing was finished. However, little progress was made on the construction. It seemed that the men from the village always had a reason not to work on it. Apparently, moose hunting was more important, and then it was too cold to work outside. By Christmas we were still in the temporary house.

The Akiak Social Scene

The teacher we were sharing our living quarters with was a first-year teacher named Christy. She was a pretty little blonde girl with a lot of enthusiasm. She only brought her clothes, a sleeping bag, and her personal items. I suppose she was thinking of this as a short-term camping trip too, or maybe she knew ahead she would be sharing a house with others.

Weather permitting, the mail plane came three days a week on Monday, Wednesday, and Friday. The post office was a tiny building that was open for a few hours on the days

My lifeline to Oregon, the Akiak post office.

the mail plane came in. Marian Jackson, a single mom with a friendly personality, was the post mistress. She helped me a lot and taught me about the native's customs, some of which included how to tan hides and do skin sewing. I actually made a beaver hat for Bob, and a couple pair of muckluks for Brendan and Treg (my two little grandsons). Muckluks are hand-sewn boots made from hides and furs. I was comfortable with the whole Jackson family, they were friendly and accepting of us from our very first meeting.

Writing and receiving mail was the only thing that kept me sane. It was my comfort from home. Every day when the mail plane came in, I was at the post office waiting for some contact from my kids, family, and friends. They never disappointed me. I can't remember a mail day that I didn't received something; a cassette tape, letter, picture, or package. One insured package from Mindy came wet and looked damaged. When I picked it up I asked Marian if I should make a claim because it was definitely damaged. I was glad she was my friend that day, All she said, was "Smell the box, it obviously has some kind of liquor in it that broke."

Because it was illegal to send alcohol through the mail, we would have been fined if it had been reported. That was the only time Mindy mailed alcohol to us. I didn't drink much before, but for some reason being in Alaska made me really enjoy a glass of wine or gin and tonic. This place was driving me to drink. Not sure exactly why, maybe the depressing weather and living conditions had something to do with it, or perhaps it was the same reason the Eskimos drank.

Alcohol was a problem for all the Kuskokwim villages. Although they were legally dry, alcohol was regularly brought in from Bethel and Anchorage. Natives paid high prices for liquor. It seemed they hadn't developed the practice of drinking socially or to just have a good time. Rather, they drank to get drunk and they were rarely pleasant or happy drunks. There was a reason the villages were legally dry. Without alcohol the Eskimo people were basically kind and law abiding. My experiences whenever I encountered natives who'd been drinking were always negative and abusive.

The Jacksons were another influential family that lived in Akiak. They were respected, active leaders in the community. Their house looked much like any house you would see in the lower 48 states. It was built up high off the ground to avoid flooding when ice in the river broke up in the spring. It was insulated and had several rooms. The 10 or 15 steps leading up to the entry and the outside had siding and fresh paint. Marian Jackson and her son lived in the family home with her parents. Her mom was one of the sweetest people I have ever met. She had severe arthritis and although her fingers were gnarled and painful, she never complained. She always had a good word and smile for everyone. Her dad, Noah Jackson, was a handsome, stately Eskimo man who seemed very wise. I can still see him walking with his walking stick through the village with his head held high and proud.

One of Marian's sisters, Helen, also lived in Akiak with her husband Jerry and their four children. Jerry was not Eskimo and had met Helen while he was in the service. They lived closer to the airstrip in a nice house that Jerry built. Jerry was the over-qualified mainte-nance man at Kuskokwim School District. He had earned a degree in psychology, but preferred to be the best maintenance man in Alaska. Helen was an awesome teacher's aide.

Weeks after our arrival in Bethel, Helen gave birth to a baby girl. I was asked to babysit for their baby Caroline and their two-year old son Alex in the mornings so that Helen could resume her position as teacher's aide. I was reluctant to babysit, because I wanted to be able to get involved in the school and village life. I agreed on the condi-tion that it would be only until she could find another sitter. Caring for those sweet babies was delightful. I learned something I had never heard of—Newborn Eskimos have a black and blue bottom. It appears to be badly bruised and if you were not aware of this ten-dency you would think the infant had been beaten. This discoloration clears up during the first few months of life.

Because I only agreed to do child care temporarily, I did not accept any pay. After a month went by and I was still babysitting, I told Helen that the next week would have to be the last day I would be available. She was able to arrange for her sister, Marian, to watch her children. The other Jackson sisters lived in Bethel and Anchorage.

The Ivan brothers and their families were more political and were members of the corporation. For some reason I never felt comfortable around them. Maybe it was because they were always so somber, and I sensed there was some resentment toward us being in their village. There was also some conflict between them and a few of the other families. We tried very hard not to get involved in the village politics.

Both Ivan families raced their dogs in the Kuskokwim 300 and the Iditarod in Nome. The Iditarod Trail Sled Dog Race is arguably the toughest race on earth. It is an annual long-distance sled-dog race held in early March between Anchorage and Nome. A team consists of mushers and 16 dogs. John Ivan also ran a little "under-the-bed" grocery store where you could buy canned goods, sometimes eggs, pilot bread which is somewhat like a soda cracker but the size of a rice cake, and spam. Their houses, like most of the other homes in the village, were wood shacks that were poorly insulated.

There were many other large families in Akiak, including the Gallela's and the Nickeri's. Most of these families also owned sled dogs. The dogs were never allowed to run at large and were not treated as pets. They were kept tied up and trained exclusively to pull sleds. It was almost majestic to see a sled team racing free across the frozen tundra. Stray dogs and dogs that could no longer work or obey their masters were shot. We witnessed a sled full of dead dogs being taken outside the village and dumped. The main diet for the dogs was fish.

They cooked most of the salmon in outside pits before feeding their dogs, but some was thrown to them fresh. I know that in Oregon and Washington we could not let our pets eat fresh salmon because it made them ill and sometimes killed them. It was interesting to learn that the lower Pacific Coast was the only location where the salmon, which was infected with a parasite, could cause death to dogs. People from the East Coast had never heard of this either.

Many of the households comprised several generations. When a teenage girl got pregnant sometimes the baby would be treated as a sibling in the household. Additionally, widowed parents or grandparents would be taken in to help with what chores they could do. Most of the social activity seemed to revolve around the church and school, especially for the young people. The villagers were quite social in the church, sharing communal meals called "The Feeds," and picking berries together on the tundra. In the summer they had blueberries (about the size of our wild huckleberries), and in the fall they had low bush cranberries and salmon berries.

The Feeds

Birthdays and special occasions were celebrated by all the villagers, including the gussocks, with a meal. Everyone in the village was invited and expected to attend. Often on the menu was a big pot of soup, usually fish or some sort of wild game. Fish soups featured a whole fish head in it. The children fought over who got the eyes. The bird soup would have feet and bills.

Along with the soup there was usually pilot bread, Jello, cake, and Eskimo ice cream. Eskimo ice cream was made with Crisco and sugar mixed with berries in season or "mouse nuts." Mouse nuts were tiny roots that mice had collected and stored underground. They would find these stores of roots, dig them, wash them, and boil them until they were tender and nut like. Sometimes the ice cream was made with seal oil. Typically, there was usually some dry fish on the table and seal oil to dip the dry fish in.

Because the houses were small and the table could only seat 6–10 at a time, you sat down when a place became available. If there was a long line of hungry people ahead of you, the wait may be more than an hour. There were never enough chairs to seat the people while they waited and it was cold outside. A common sight was of many older women sitting cross legged on the floor and leaning against a wall or sitting on five-gallon buckets. Waiting was a time to visit and get to know each other a little better.

At my first feed, I ate everything served to me to be polite, and when the hostess asked me how I liked the ice cream, I told a white lie and said it was good. The next day she came to visit and brought me a butter tub filled with left over ice cream. I said "thank you" and began to put it in my ice chest to keep cool. Marian said, "Oh, let's have some now." Right then I knew telling the truth would have been the better choice. There was always Eskimo ice cream and I did eat it, but never acquired a taste for it.

The second year in the village the school bought a soft ice cream maker. The Eskimos loved real ice cream and paid 75 cents for a cone. This turned out to be a money maker at social events. The machine would run out before everyone had their fill of ice cream. Making and cleaning the machine became the staff's duties. I don't think any of us enjoyed that part of it.

A large amount of interaction occurred between the villages that were close in proximity to one another. Travel for sports events was either by plane and four wheeler or snow machine and sled in the winter. Overall, the Yup'ik people were friendly and peace loving. Everyone seemed happy and amiable at the feeds and social events at the school. The young adults often fell in love and married between villages. Couples would move to the village to which they both felt more at home. Sometimes they would live with parents until they were able to build a place of their own.

Fitting in

Some of the natives referred to me as the tall, skinny *gussock*. Never in my 44 years had I been called tall. Although we didn't have much in common, I was beginning to like these people. For the most part, they were short and sturdily built with beautiful skin, dark brown eyes, and black hair. It was difficult to tell the age of the adults. They seemed ageless to me.

Still, after a few weeks in the village, it was clear to me that living in Alaska was nothing like I had imagined. I had hoped it would be more romantic. Bob and I living in a log cabin out on the tundra like the people living on the prairie 50 years ago. Instead, although there was plenty of people around, I felt isolated from everything I knew.

Settling into our living situation was also a challenge. Everything took longer to do without modern conveniences. There is no way I could have survived there without Bob. He was my protector and he worked so hard to make things easier for me. Despite the full days of preparing lesson plans and teaching, plus coaching sports events and extracurricular activities for the kids, there was always a honey-do list when he came home—water to be hauled to our garbage can, a new oil barrel hooked up for our heat, curtains to be hung. He missed his kids as much as I did, but he was always there to cheer me up with one of his funny stories or a fantastic idea about what we would do in the summer. We played a lot of card games and read a lot. It was always a fun time to share our tapes and letters from our kids after a day at school.

Likewise, in addition to adjusting to our new surroundings, I was also struggling to accept how these people lived, often comparing it to where I had lived. It seemed outrageous to have so much abuse and for the women in the village to deal with so much hardship. Bob had more insight into their culture and how it was evolving. We often had discussions about why something wasn't being done to stop this behavior. Bob would say things like, "this kind of behavior happens in every culture. It happens in Springfield still to this day. We just are not as aware or as close to it. Akiak is a small village and everybody knows what goes on. It takes time for cultures to evolve. In time things will get better for them."

And then there was the language barrier. According to most experts, the Yup'ik language is the most commonly used native language in North America. It is the first language spoken by most of the native Alaskan people. Yup'ik was their first language, but the children spoke some English. A few of the older residents did not understand or speak English at all. The Yup'ik language is almost always accompanied by a lot of gestures and is very guttural. Some of the words sounded obscene; especially when I tried to say them. The Yup'ik languages were not written until the arrival of Europeans around the beginning of the 19th century. The earliest efforts at writing Yup'ik were those of missionaries who, with their Yup'ik-speaking assistants, translated the Bible and other religious texts into Yup'ik.

While we were in the villages there were no printed newspapers, magazines, or story books written in Yup'ik. Yup'ik does not distinguish between gender, thus the children had a hard time with "he and she". The teacher aides were very helpful with translation for the younger students.

Even body language was different, as were standards for politeness. I learned that raising your eyebrows meant "yes," a shake of the head was "no", and if you asked a question a person didn't want to answer, they ignored you rather than offer a refusal or explanation. Until recent generations, the Yup'ik people had lived almost exclusively in communal housing. Traditionally, all the men and boys lived in a single large building that also served as the gathering space for community events. The women lived in smaller group houses. Privacy is still not a well-developed concept among the Yup'ik. With a front door that wouldn't lock, people could (and did) walk into our house any time. I told the kids that they couldn't visit unless they knocked on the door and I had asked them to come in.

When the adults and kids came to visit, they would often sit and not say anything. I was very uncomfortable with this so I'd ask questions or offer them food or drink, until I learned they thought I was nervous and talked too much. The kids were happy simply to be inside where it was safe and warm.

I got along well with the children, they taught me some Yup'ik. We made cookies, tried our hand at some crafts, and just hung out. When

Bob was home we played games. Cribbage was a favorite. That was one card game almost all the kids knew how to play and they were good at it. When Bob and I played he usually won.

If I won it was luck and when he won it was all skill. For a while, we kept score of who won and lost. During that period of time I won more than he did and that proved, according to him, that Cribbage was merely a game of luck!

Communicating with the adults was different. Our conversations were limited to the weather and what was happening in the village. We had nothing in common. One day, Helena came to visit and noticed some cleaned birds in my arctic porch. She said, "Oh Bob got some birds. Who cleaned them?" I told her that Bob had and her reply was, "with his hands"? A few weeks later she told a group of people waiting to eat at one of the feeds that Bob has to clean his own birds and they then proceeded to tell me that "that was not the way to do things. Here the women clean and prepare the fish and game. Husbands only hunt and fish."

For the most part, the women bore the major responsibility of labor. Historically, the division of labor between the sexes was probably more equitable, but they haven't really adjusted to how much easier the traditional male role of providing game and fish has become.

I learned that so many of the customs were different from what I was used to. Fishing and hunting is a sport in Oregon and the division of labor is shared. Usually, whoever catches it, cleans it. In fact it took years for Bob to teach me how to gut a fish that I had caught, not because I was such a slow learner, but because it was a job I didn't want to learn.

Another difference I found amusing was when I planned a bridal shower for one of the girls in the village who was getting married. The guests showed up with soaps and towels, thinking it was literally a "shower." They took many of the things I said literally. Their customs fit their living conditions and lifestyles while mine were from a whole different time period and environment .

The Eskimo women all liked Bob. He spent time with the women, cutting up fish and learning all their methods of making dry fish. He tasted their seal oil, stink head, etc. Bob was comfortable with this culture and was beginning to love the Eskimo people. This was one of his subtle ways to show the young men in the village it was okay to do "women's work." I, on the other hand, wasn't nearly so subtle, and was having a hard time with their culture.

The School

The Molly Hooch Act had gone into effect shortly before we arrived in Alaska. It was a good thing to end the practice of sending children off to boarding school after eighth grade, but the transition from

Bob outside his classroom in Akiak.

a program that had been ongoing for decades wasn't without issues. Parents were at a loss to know how to raise teenagers. There were few people in the village who'd raised teens, or even been teens themselves in a village setting. The law now allowed the teens to stay in the villages, but they wanted dances, parties, and activities like other teens. For the most part, these things hadn't been planned or weren't available in the village.

The state school building in Akiak housed K–12. It had a well and plumbing, which allowed it to have running water, flush toilets, and showers. It had laundry facilities and a full kitchen to serve breakfast and lunch to the students. We couldn't have survived without the use of the shower, the washer and dryer, and the oven in the kitchen. Teachers were allowed to carry water from the school for use at their homes and to use the laundry facilities and kitchen on weekends. The natives carried water from the river. The river water looked so clear and tasted so much better that one winter we tried switching to it. I became ill shortly after drinking it. The visiting physician (Dr. Nice) on his regular visit confirmed that I had contracted Giardia from the river water. We went back to the rusty water.

Bob and Carlson taught the high school students and Christy taught the entire elementary until another teacher was hired in December. I was hired to teach the home economics class and sub for teachers, the school cook, and secretary when needed. The teacher aides, school secretary, cook, janitor and maintenance man were all local residents of Akiak. Matt Gillella, the school secretary, was a charming young man who had gone to high school in Oregon and spoke perfect English.

This was the first year the school received several Apple computers, which was not something Bob was experienced with. It became Bob's job to set up these computers and keep them in operation, plus teach the students how to use them. He spent some time learning Computers 101 in a hurry.

The school gym was the social gathering place for many activities. Akiak was big on indoor sports; basketball, wrestling, and volleyball. Bob coached the wrestlers and Carlton and Matt coached basketball and volleyball that first year. When there was a game at the school, the whole village came out to watch. They sat on benches around the outside of the playing floor and cheered on their favorite team. Many of the people chewed tobacco and they would use paper cups or empty bottles to spit in. After an event there was always a mess of tobacco-filled containers to clean up.

The children in the village were sweet and naïve. Not as worldly as the teens in the bigger cities. Most of what they knew about gussocks, and life in the lower 48, they learned from television and magazines. Not always a model of reality. They loved music and it was a typical sight to see them with a boom box blaring popular music.

Holidays

The first year we were in Akiak we celebrated Bob's Birthday in October by inviting all the high school kids over for cake and home-made ice cream. They were so excited to share that day with Bob and it helped make the day easier for him. We had always celebrated it as the "Big Birthday" because two of his grandsons and a daughter-in-law shared the same birthday on the 9th. We played games, sang songs, and Bob did some magic tricks that included a hair dancing in a bowl of water. When the kids put their faces down to see the hair dance, Bob splashed the water, which made the hair dance, but also got the kids and the floor wet.

Halloween was a fun time for everyone in the village. Much like mid-winter weather in Oregon, there was usually snow and cold weather in Akiak by the end of October. The children, adults, and even grandparents dressed up in costume and went house to house trick-or-treating. They gathered at the first house and then went out as a group. When it was your house, you went in and passed out the treats. Sometimes it took hours to go to every house. If the house had two doors, you would go in one and out the other.

A Russian Orthodox church.

Jerry and Helen Keller invited us to spend our first Thanksgiving in Akiak with their family. I especially enjoyed helping cook the dinner. Thanksgiving Day has always been one of my favorite family holidays, and that year it was doubly special because it was also my birthday and we had new friends to celebrate with.

Christmas was celebrated at the Moravian Church with beautiful singing and a reenactment of the Christmas story. They had a traditional Russian Orthodox Slovak celebration in January where they visited every house in the village, blessing them with prayer and song. The host family handed out snacks and small gifts. It took several days and nights to bless all the houses in the village. Sometimes other villagers would join the celebration. Akiak did not have a Russian Orthodox Church, but they observed this tradition.

In February, the Kuskokwim 300 dog-sled race was held. Every year the dog-sled teams stopped in Akiak to rest and refresh their teams. School was dismissed and almost everyone came out to cheer the racers on. The kids from my home economics class prepared snacks and hot chocolate for the racers. It was interesting to see how well trained the sled dogs were and how they depended on the lead dog. Some of the dogs had booties to keep their paws warm.

Easter was always a village-wide holiday. We rose before dawn, bundled in our warmest parka and boots and walked to the cemetery for a sunrise service of prayer and singing to celebrate that Jesus has risen. The rest of the day was spent going from house to house and eating. It was a day of friendship and sharing. It was also the day Helena shared the fact that I didn't clean and prepare the fish and wild game Bob brought home.

Teaching and the Village Kids

Although I didn't possess a teaching certificate, I was asked to teach the home economics class one hour in the afternoon, and substitute for other teachers when needed. My lack of experience subbing the junior high classes was challenging. I had little control of that classroom. Sometimes I felt like I was in the jungle with wild animals.

Teaching the home economics class was a bright spot for me that first year. I had eight young girls in my class and our first project was sewing. Sewing machines were not available in most homes, because most of their sewing was hand sewing. Our first few weeks were spent learning about the electric sewing machine. Because we only had four Bernina sewing machines they worked with partners. The first sewing project was making an apron. They were proud of their accomplishments and eager to do something more difficult, so their next project was to pick out a dress pattern, cut it out and sew it. They were so willing to learn and fun to teach. When their dresses were finished we put on a fashion show and they posed for pictures.

The next semester we did cooking. A couple of boys signed up for this class too, so we started with very simple foods like breakfast and snacks. As they got comfortable with these things we graduated to baking and meal planning.

A typical social function in the school gymnasium, the center of village life.

One thing I wanted to impress upon the young people, especially the girls, was that along with an education came options. They could be anything they aspired to be. They could, but didn't have to settle for living the life of their mothers and they certainly didn't have to put up with being abused. They could go out and see the world. It would be their choice if they decided to come back to the village or make a life somewhere else. If they chose to come back to the village they could be the teachers, nurses, lawyers, doctors, or whatever they chose and they could make life better for their families.

One of the things that was most upsetting about daily life in the village was the large amount of alcoholism, abuse, incest, and violent death for such a small population. Our house was often filled with kids coming to "visit"—many of them just wanting to be safe, especially when there was drinking going on in their homes.

It was a nearly every-day occurrence to have kids knock on the door and want to visit. This was unfamiliar behavior to me. Ordinarily kids who came to my house wanted to play with my children. Why were they so intent on visiting a total adult stranger? I thought at first it was curiosity, but they never asked questions, so I figured it was a place of refuge for them.

One young boy was found dead sniffing gasoline. Several of the older children sniffed gas to get high. That may have had some bearing on the fact there was a large percentage of special education students in the villages.

One of the little girls that still tugs at my heart strings was little Nettie. I first met her when she was five, a barefoot little girl with rosy checks, a big smile and green elevens (what a runny nose was referred to in my family). She was old beyond her years. She wore a pair of jeans with a circle marked in her back pocket where she carried a can of snuff. That little girl at five could swear like a logger and spit farther than most men. Nettie had been exposed to the worst home life imaginable. Her brother, Emile, was beaten so badly by their father one night that he was unrecognizable when they took him to the hospital. The father was arrested and taken into custody. A few days later before his son's physical wounds healed, he was back in the village.

Bob was always careful not to antagonize or interfere with anyone who had been drinking lest they become very belligerent and mean. He bent over backwards to appease them and keep the peace. One evening there was a knock on our door around 8:30. Two very intoxicated strangers said they were on their way to Akiachak, a village about 10 miles from Akiak, couldn't find the trail, saw our light and needed directions. Bob tried to get them to go to an Eskimo house because he didn't know how to direct them.

One of the guys was trying to get in the room and touch me, saying he wanted to kiss me. Bob tried his hardest to get them to leave without making them angry. Most carry guns or at least a hunting knife so it is better to stay cool and gently guide them away. While he was doing this one leaned over and his nasty breath almost knocked me out. Nelson, one of our students was visiting us when this was taking place. He immediately ran to get the village police. They left before the police arrived. Often we would hear children screaming in the night. Instinctively, you would want to go help them, but we were told not to interfere. It could be dangerous. We were the minority.

Living Arrangements

While we continued to wait for teacher housing to be built, sharing living space with Christy, the young, naïve first-year teacher became increasingly difficult. We split the rent three ways, plus other expenses and food and heating, and a 50-gallon oil tank lasted five to seven days some months, making our heat bill almost as much as our rent. The young men in the village were attracted to this cute, little blonde girl with a job. She fell into their trap and shortly after arriving in the village she started dating.

Occasionally, one of these boy "friends" would spend the night with her on the couch. I have never been accused of being a prude, but being exposed to their nighttime activities made me uncomfortable. At one point, she asked if her new boyfriend Tim could move in and she would pay half the rent. It was a definite "no" from both Bob and I. I could not imagine having this angry alcoholic teenager in my space in the morning when Bob and Christy had gone to school. After that, she started sleeping at Tim's house, sharing a bottom bunk in a bedroom with Tim and his 10-year-old brother. She came back in the mornings to eat breakfast and get ready for school, but spent very little time with us. I never knew if she would be there to eat dinner with us or not.

Tim was the landlord's son. In November, the landlord asked Bob if his son could move in with Christy for the three weeks in December when we would be going home for Christmas. He said his family would like to have a nice Christmas and with Christy sleeping there it was very uncomfortable for his wife and other children. Looking back, this was another difference in our culture that I didn't understand at the time. The parents were afraid of alienating their children, fearing their anger and that they may break away from the family. We agreed to let Tim stay there in our absence.

It started years ago, Bob's family had a traditional Christmas gag gift, a fungus (huge tree conk). Every Christmas someone in the family would receive this gift-wrapped fungus with a note about why they deserved it. Because Bob had gotten it the Christmas before, he packed it to Alaska in case we didn't get home for the holidays and he would mail it to Oregon with his letter. It had been sitting on our kitchen table, but when we were getting ready to go home for the holidays it had disappeared. We learned later that some of the conks in Alaska had the same hallucinogenic effect as some mushrooms when ingested or smoked. The missing fungus was never found. Possibly it ended up in someone's pipe.

We arrived in Springfield several days before Christmas giving us time to do some shopping, baking, decorating the tree, and just being with our loved ones. Because the people in Akiak celebrated Slavic, (a Russian Orthodox celebration, which took place a couple weeks after Christmas) school was closed for three weeks. Those three weeks were like the best vacation ever.

Finally, our teacher's housing place in Akiak.

Upon returning to Akiak after spending a wonderful holiday with our children in Oregon, we found a lock on the door and a newly hired teacher with large dogs living in the house along with Christy and Tim. We could not get into the house and retrieve any of our belongings. Although he lived in a small shack with only a twin bed, table and chairs, a small counter with a hot plate, and a honey bucket, Carlton, the school principal, graciously allowed Bob and I to stay with him for about six weeks until our house was finished in February. Bob and I slept on the twin bed and Carlton slept in a sleeping bag on the floor. We lived out of what we had in our suitcases. Our Springfield neighbor Marvin had given us a bottle of "Pina Coladas for Two" to take back with us at Christmas. Although it was well padded among our clothes, it broke and everything in the suitcase smelled like coconut.

In February, our house was finally finished and we were able to move in, but we faced another hurdle trying to retrieve our belongings. There was always an excuse or reason why we couldn't go in and get our stuff. They had the dogs in the house and were not cooperative about giving us a time when they would put the dogs out.

Finally, the new teacher's boyfriend came to Akiak and they moved into an empty shack with their sled dogs. She was only in the village for the remainder of the school year. Seems her boyfriend was from an area where they ate dog meat. One of their dogs was sick so they killed it and they had the dog meat drying behind their oil heater. It was acceptable to eat dog meat in the area where he came from so they didn't realize it would become a problem in this Yupik village. The Yupik Eskimo do not eat dog meat and they were asked to leave.

When we finally were allowed into the house to retrieve our things, I was devastated to see what had become of our meager belongings. Clothes, bedding, and appliances were all piled in the middle of the room. Our radio/tape player was broken. Christy said Tim had thrown it at her in one of his drunken rages. There were dirty dishes in frozen dishwater in our dishpan. Many of our plastic plates were burned on the bottom where they had been set on the coils of the hot plate. Our pots and pans were crusty and probably used as dog dishes.

Things were missing and everything that was there was a mess. To cart all this stuff to the school, clean it up and take it to our new dwelling was a nightmare. Still, I was excited at the prospect of moving into our first new home, a home with two small bedrooms, no closets, but an actual bed with a mattress. It had a bathroom with a honey bucket and a great room. We had a couch, table and benches, a hot plate and refrigerator, with a promise of an electric range and freezer for the next school year!

The End of the First Hard Year

In 1967, North America's largest oil reserve was discovered on jointly owned land in Alaska's North Slope. In 1976, the state amended its constitution to dedicate a part of its yearly oil revenues to a state investment fund, called the Alaska Permanent Fund. The goal of the fund was to ensure that every Alaskan would benefit from the state's decision to exploit its oil resources and that they could continue to benefit even after oil production ended. For the first six years the state let the fund accrue without spending any of its returns. Since 1982, Alaskans have received that yearly dividend. The amount varies year to year depending on a complex formula. The PFD has been between $1,000 and $1,500 per person, which was almost enough money to last the winter for a large family. After one year's residency in Alaska we received our permanent fund check every fall.

Although living in the bush was hard, being so far from my children was the hardest. Many dreary days I walked alone through the woods and down by the river and pretended I was somewhere else . . . London, or on an exotic island. I cried a lot that first year. You know you are homesick when:

- The highlight of your day is checking the thermometer to see how cold it is;

- Your best friend is a tape recorder and a spiral notebook;

- You live for 3:30 p.m. every Monday, Wednesday and Friday—the days the mail plane comes;

- Paying the bills from Oregon is a pleasure;

- You can sit alone in a darkened room at 4:00 in the afternoon with tears running down your face not giving a damn if anyone sees;

- You start to plan, not for each day, but instead for Christmas or May, whichever comes first.

But then I would get a letter or a tape from home and my world would be good again. In one letter my son Jason sent me a fake check for a million dollars. Money can't buy happiness, but my sweet broke college student made me laugh. We were sending him money every month to go to school.

Being so many miles away from home was a constant worry for me. If I didn't hear from my kids for a week I imagined all kinds of things. I treasured all their short letters and funny tapes, telling us about school, adventures, trips to the fair where Aaron had won a stuffed carrot. One letter said my daughter Mindy was sick for a long time and they were worried about her. I guessed she might be pregnant and it turned out to be right. Baby Brendan was on the way.

School in Alaska was out in early May at breakup. As soon as the ice started to flow it was time for fishing and school was over. They had a contest when the first ice started to move. They actually had a setup that would alert them when the ice moved and the closest guess was the winner. I don't remember what the prize was or if I ever knew. Usually we were on our way home before breakup. Some years there would be an ice jam and the water would flood the village. When we came back in the fall, there were trenches where the ice had come up and dug out a path. They told stories about how they were stranded in their houses for days because the water was so high. Once they had to be evacuated and taken to Bethel by plane to get drinking water.

By the time spring came and my nine months were up, we had our own little cabin close to the school. I had learned a lot from the natives, liked working with the children at the school, and felt confident that my own children were doing okay without me. When Bob said he needed to work at least another year to make his resume sound good, I agreed to another year. Besides, the long awaited summer vacation was nearly here and I was going to have three whole months of living in the beautiful state of Oregon.

Going Home for the Summer

Our plane landed at the Portland airport just moments after our grandson Brendan was born in Eugene. We did get home in time for Aaron's High School graduation, but had to be content with seeing pictures of his senior prom.

Jeff, his wife Susan, and their baby Joshua were living in California. Jeff planned to move back to Oregon with his family and live in our house while we were away. This seemed an ideal arrangement and we spent part of our summer making the house safe for a two year old.

The saddest part of homecoming was when we learned our beautiful Norwegian Elk hound Odin had to be put down. A couple of loose dogs, a Pit Bull and Doberman, attacked him in our yard. A neighbor turned the hose on them, got Odin out from under the car in our driveway, and took him to the vet. Two vets worked on him all night and called Mindy the next morning to say that to save Odin's life they would have to amputate one of his front legs. This was Mother's Day weekend and Mindy was due to have her baby any day. She couldn't make that decision by herself. She called Jason in Corvallis and he said, "Have him put down." We not only lost our favorite pet, but also had a huge vet bill to pay.

The summer was always too short. Time to catch up on what was going on with our children, family, and friends, and lots of picnics, traveling, visiting, and shopping for supplies for the next school year. Every summer we planned a girl's shopping trip. My sisters Patty and

Tillie, sister-in-law Linda, and my daughter Mindy and I would go for two or three days to shop and play either to the coast or sometimes Seattle. My lifelong friend Joan also went on a few of our coastal shopping trips. We had plans to go to San Francisco, but like the tropical island that never happened. Our trips here were great. We shopped until we dropped and then spent some relaxing time by a pool with a glass of wine. On one trip, we rode the train to Seattle and took a limo back and forth to our hotel after shopping. We always had so much fun. I miss those days.

Our next-door neighbors in Springfield were Marvin Hall and his sweet mother. Mrs. Hall was a delightful older woman, a bit of an alcoholic, but she never came out of her house without makeup. She wore bright red lipstick, had jet-black dyed hair, and penciled-in eyebrows to match her hair. She read trashy scandal magazines and knew all about the lives of Hollywood movie stars. And she loved my kids and grandkids. She had agates in the walkway to her house. Brendan and Joshua would sit by her walkway and point to their favorite ones. One day I saw Mrs. Hall out there with a screwdriver breaking out the agates and giving them to the boys.

Marvin was another story. He was a war veteran and lived in a small camp trailer on his parent's property. He thought the sun rose and set on me for some reason. Maybe it was because he was an alcoholic and had a little brain damage. He brought me watermelon, berries, and vegetables from his garden when I was in my backyard. He liked to play blackjack for quarters, and although we spent many afternoons playing he never went home with any of my quarters. It wasn't because I always won. If I was losing he would make a bad bet and lose before he went home. Sometimes he just bought us pizza for dinner with his winnings. He called me Little Mama and according to him I could do no wrong. Bob was Big Daddy and he loved my little granddaughter Dani, and liked to bring her things.

One day he brought her a footlocker with a $2 bill inside. Never did understand why a footlocker, but it was a good place to store some of her toys. Sometimes, he could be annoying. Like the time he was here playing blackjack and had his fifth of whiskey in his pocket. I never gave him any alcoholic beverages. By the time he wanted to get up and go home, he couldn't stand by himself. Jason helped him get into his trailer. He didn't want to have his mom see him drunk so they had to go around the back yard and over the fence. When Jason got him home he dumped the rest of his bottle out on the ground. The next day Marvin was back trying to find his bottle of whiskey. He remembered that there was still some left.

Despite his shortcomings, Marvin was terrific about sending me amusing letters from home, candy, scandal magazines, gossip about the neighborhood, and in particular, what was going on at my house next door.

Second year (Akiak) and Beyond

Three new teachers were hired for the 81–82 school year. Another high school teacher was hired to free up the principal, and a special education teacher position was added to the staff, plus filling the position of elementary teacher who had left at the end of the first year. Bill was the English and shop teacher. Two new houses were being built right next to the school. Bill bunked with us until his house was finished. He was handsome, charismatic, and charming.

The other teachers were mirror image twins from the east coast, Kathy and Debbie. Beautiful redheads. Kathy was the special education

Bill, Debbie, Bob, and the author, year two.

teacher and Debbie taught elementary. They were personality plus and made every day living in the bush an adventure. It was so nice to have these new friends to share our life with. Kathy and Debbie bunked with Carlton until their teacher house was built. The natives built two small teacher houses in front of the school building, and the school district furnished them. They had actual store-bought tables and chairs, beds, and couches. I was jealous.

Christy had married her boyfriend and had a baby boy. Life was very hard for her this second year trying to raise the baby, teach school, and keep her house warm. Her husband spent a lot of time away, leaving her alone to cope in the harsh winter. They had a wood stove for heating and sometimes she was left without split firewood. On occasion, she would come to school with bruises and her job performance deteriorated to the point she was laid off. Christy was raised in Alaska. I don't remember what city, but her mother came to the village and moved Christy and the baby home with her, which was not well accepted by the villagers.

This year, Bill, Kathy, Debbie, Bob and I did so much together that we almost seemed like one big family. We prepared and ate dinner together almost every night. Sometimes Debbie would take the dirty dishes to the school and wash them. We didn't know at the time but she had an ulterior motive for going to the school after meals.

We had a small television and many evenings we would all sit

Bob and his snow machine.

on our bed and watch TV. The programs were something else. You could sponsor a program and they would broadcast it. For a few months someone sponsored the Tonight Show and it came on at 8:00 p.m.. Television was on the air usually from five to 11. Sometimes they would show a movie and if it lasted longer than the shut off time, you would never see the end. One time they played the second reel first, and another time we saw the second reel upside down. It was entertainment in itself. Many of our discussions were marathons about what color was the icing on the cake, a lyric in the Richard Harris song "MacArthur Park." We didn't have smart phones to give us the answers to our discussions. In fact, we didn't even have phones.

Weekends were spent snow machine riding. Bill, Bob, and sometimes the twins would go out and gather firewood for heat. I usually stayed home and baked bread and did laundry while they chopped wood. We took long walks on the tundra and across the frozen river. When it was too miserable to walk outside we could exercise in the gym. Moses, a jolly old Eskimo man lived in a house across the river. He worked at the school as a janitor and would cross the river by boat until it was frozen, then he came by snow machine. There was only a short time during the year that he couldn't navigate the river safely. At one time there were Laplanders with reindeer herds living across the river. They built and lived in the cutest homes.

One day we walked across the river and had coffee with Moses. He showed us his treasures— a beautiful stuffed eagle, bear paws, and the neatest woodpile in the whole state of Alaska. Evidently, Moses' wife ran off with the Laplander who had built this house.

I helped him fill out a form for something one day and the question asked (married, single, divorced) his answer was "I don't know." She had left many years ago and he didn't know if she divorced him or not or even if she was still alive. A few years after we left the village I heard that Moses had died when his snow machine had fallen through the ice.

Bob was a terrific teacher and had a way with working with even the most difficult child. He would pick the most disruptive kid in class and make him or her his assistant. Before long, that was the kid that tried the hardest. Sometimes he called the girls Gladys and for some reason they loved it. Little did they know it was at times when he couldn't remember their names. In the end it served as a term of endearment and they all liked to be called Gladys. He did a lot of science projects with the students. One demonstration was in a classroom when I was subbing for sixth and seventh graders. He had frozen dog eyeballs and they were dissecting them. The kids had picks to look at the layers. One kid was picking his teeth with the pick. Grossed me out!

Bob made arrangements with a teacher in Eugene who taught sixth graders to correspond with his ninth graders. Some of the letters were adorable. Actually, they seemed to be on about the same grade level with their writing. One student was so insulted that the kids in Eugene thought they still lived in igloos that he responded with, "Our igloo burned down so we are now living in a wooden house."

Teaching the home economics class was becoming more fun than ever. Carlton was great. He allowed me free rein with my endeavors. My cooking class opened a bakery. The first week they concentrated on breads, cinnamon rolls, and muffins. They baked the products ahead of time, packaged them, and froze them until the day their bakery was open. They advertised what time and day the bakery would be open and what products would be for sale. On the day of the sale they set out their baked goods on a table in the gym, priced everything, and when they opened the doors they sold out within minutes. The parents were happy to get fresh baked goods and the students were delighted to show off their baking skills. An added lesson was they had to make change and keep a record of their earnings. They didn't have to pay the school for the supplies, so all the money could be kept for field trips.

This second year we were in the village, Marian's mother was in the hospital. Noah went to take a steam bath the night before going to visit his wife. He was gone a long time and when his grandson Sammy, went to check on him, he was found dead. Apparently he had a heart attack, tried to get out, but fell by the door. It was such a sad day for the village.

The cemetery was in the outskirts of the village. It had little fences around the family plots. If someone died during the winter their body had to be stored in a frozen state until the ground was thawed enough to dig the grave.

I only attended one funeral service while I was in Akiak. Noah Jackson's body was kept cool awaiting the coffin that was being sent from Anchorage. There was a service in the house before the coffin arrived. Noah was on a blanket on the living room floor. People came from many villages as Noah was well known and loved by many. For the three days of the service the family prepared food for the travelers, and the service was held in their home.

Forty days after a death they had another celebration of life for their loved one. Hundreds of people came for this singing, praying, eating, and remembering the dead. If the burial was to be somewhere outside the village, the corpse would be put in a sitting position so when rigor mortis set in it could be transported in a bush plane. This is what one Eskimo told me. It sort of made sense at the time, but I am not sure it really happened.

Before the teachers all left for the Christmas holiday, we had a program

The cemetary in Akiak.

at the school. One year, Bill had his English class rewrite *A Christmas Carol* to reflect life in the village and the students performed the play. The younger students did skits and sang carols. We all enjoyed hearing those little voices singing in both English and Yup'ik.

To save some money that second year Bob and I decided to spend Christmas in the village. Traveling during December was hectic and our vacation time was shorter than the year before. Bill, Debbie, and Kathy all left for their hometowns. We were feeling pretty lonely, planning our meager canned spam Christmas dinner, but then, like a Christmas miracle, a plane landed and Kathy and Debbie came in laden with gifts and food.

Their flight to New England was cancelled because of weather and they decided not to wait around the airport to catch another flight if the weather improved. They came back to spend Christmas with us. They brought presents, decorations, and a wonderful Christmas dinner. We had such a joyful celebration with these loving girls. When Bill came back from his Christmas vacation he brought me a kitchen sink and built it into my house. Now I could wash dishes in a real sink. It didn't have a faucet, but it had a drain and a large bucket underneath. I loved it. Bill also made me a little end table and a small chest to hold magazines.

Things were getting better and better. Every time we moved I took those two pieces of furniture with me. I still have them. Precious reminders of our friendships those years in Alaska. Bill encouraged me to keep a journal. My spiral notebook served as a faithful companion during my years in Alaska. Bill was an excellent English teacher and encouraged his students to write. I have a book of his poetry that I often read with fond memories.

Snow Mishaps

One Saturday, Carlton was going into Bethel to get some groceries and gas for the snow machines. Kathy and I went along riding in the sled. There were times when you just had to have green grapes or any type of fresh fruit, and a day's trip to Bethel would be worth the discomfort. Although we were dressed warmly in Parkas, snow boots, gloves, and hats, the additional blankets felt good. Imagine riding 30 miles sitting in a wooden sled being pulled by a snow machine bouncing around on the ice. Not a very pleasant or comfortable ride. Additionally, I was always afraid of going through the ice or getting lost.

After we did our shopping we were packed in the sled with our supplies and began our long journey home. Not sure how far we were from the village when our sled came to a stop and Carlton couldn't fix the problem with his snow machine. It was dark, cold and I thought we were lost on the tundra. We left everything in the sled and started walking. I don't know how Carlton knew where the trail went. His only light was a flashlight. Sometimes I would get off the trail and the snow would cover my boots. It seemed like 100 miles. My legs were so cold and tired trudging through the snow that I just wanted to lie down and rest, but of course I had heard many stories about freezing to death so I kept on walking. Besides, Carlton made me keep walking. He said no way would he be responsible for letting anything happen to me. Bob would kill him.

Our little cabin never looked so good when we finally got home. The next day, Bob drove Carlton out to repair his machine and retrieve the sled and all our groceries. Usually I was the one at home worrying about Bob when he was out on his snow machine. Nothing was worth this trip to Bethel. The green grapes were not fresh when we got them the next day, they were frozen.

Hunting ptarmigon, a medium-sized gamebird in the grouse family, was supposed to be easy. They have a natural camouflage. In winter they turn snow white and in the summer they are the color of the woods where they live. Maybe they feel secure because they blend in with the environment or they may just be stupid. However, you can get close enough to sometimes knock them out with a tennis racket. One weekend a group of teachers and some students and their dads went out to hunt ptarmigan. Bob came home with a sack full of birds and a shotgun pellet in his leg. Someone had shot at a bird, but the shot hit Bob and another young man. Their heavy parkas repelled some of the shot, but one penetrated Bob's jeans and lodged in his lower leg. Bob grew up with a mother who stitched up his wounds. This was not my calling. Under the circumstances I got a sterile knife, some bandages, rubbing alcohol, and because there was only a little whiskey left in our house, I knew it was not enough to help Bob, so I drank it. The operation was a success! The other victim went to the out-patient hospital in Bethel to get his removed.

The BIA hospital in Bethel was free to the natives, but they would help us only if it was an emergency. Once a week a doctor at the Family Clinic in Bethel would see us there if we had a health problem. Each village had a clinic staffed by a resident. She was trained in first aid and had phone access to a doctor from the hospital. When someone came in with a complaint, she took their temperature, blood pressure, and phoned the complaints and patient's stats to the doctor who would prescribe treatment. Medications were flown out with the next plane. The clinic had a supply of antibiotics and some common medications and bandages. Seemed like every child with a runny nose got antibiotics.

Village Culture

A 12-year-old girl told the special education teacher that she was molested by an uncle while her mother was out of town. She was staying with the aunt and uncle during her mother's absence. The special education teacher reported the incident to the Social Services Department in Bethel. They responded to her written report over the Tundra Drums. The Tundra Drums was a communication system via radio that was broadcast morning and evening with messages that were heard by everyone.

The teacher's report to the authorities did not sit well with the family. Even the girl's mother was upset that a report was made. The adults felt it was the girl's problem because of her behavior. Anyway, the Special Ed teacher was almost tarred and feathered for her efforts. In many ways the end result was positive for the young girl. She trusted her teacher and they became close friends. This girl was extremely bright and talented. With the help of this special teacher she finished school in the village, went on to college, left the village, and became a teacher. For some reason, many mothers were in denial or just looked the other way. Maybe it was because that is how it was when they were growing up or perhaps because they felt powerless around men. Children in the villages grew up way too fast. A large percentage of young girls were abused before the age of 12.

There were many superstitions; some as simple as not leaving your shoes in front of the door at night. If you did, some spirit would come and dance in your shoes and you wouldn't be able to find them in the morning. My favorite one was the red-eyed woman. If she looked you in the eye it was because you were next in line to die. Never whistle at the northern lights. They may strike you dead. Cats were feared and I am not sure why.

More Snow Mishaps

It was always dangerous to travel any distance by snow machine. You never knew when an emergency would arise, a breakdown, you might run out of gas, get lost, or get stuck in a whiteout. On one winter weekend Bill, Debbie, and Kathy took off for Bethel with their sled and two snow machines. Bill drove one and pulled the sled and Kathy drove the other.

They had planned to come back the same day; however, there was a storm warning late in the afternoon and we thought they had stayed in town to wait out the storm. We weren't too concerned until Sunday afternoon when we found out they had left early Saturday afternoon. My rosary beads were getting a workout. It was a total white out, but as soon as it cleared enough searchers went out to find them. The weather was still too bad for search planes until Monday.

A young man named Moses found them from the fire they had built. By this time they were suffering from exposure and probably could not have survived much longer. They had food that they bought in Bethel and matches so they could build a fire for heat. They had to leave their tank of gas along the trail because the sled kept getting stuck in the snow. They ended up miles in the wrong direction. It was good that they didn't have the extra gas with them. They might have gone even farther in the wrong direction and it would have been harder to find them.

When they staggered into the village from the airstrip they were a pathetic trio. They had burned their boots and were wearing garbage bags on their feet. Everyone was so happy to see them and hear their version of the adventure. They gave Bob some of the credit for their survival in the extreme weather. They were raised mostly in the city and Bob had shown them many ways to survive in the wilderness.

Visiting Artists

A program called, "Artists in the School" was formed in 1966 to ensure that the role of arts in the life of the communities will continue to grow and play a significant part in the welfare and educational experience of Alaskan citizens. This program is supported by the State of Alaska and the National Endowment for the Arts. Funds are granted and services provided by the Alaskan State Legislature.

We were lucky to have two talented performers spend two weeks in our village each year. Dana and Jane were two of my favorites. They were both talented musicians, singers, and performers who worked with the students and teachers on musical performance, play acting and writing, making sets, etc. Dana had a beautiful Irish tenor voice and performed in many theaters and pubs in the lower 48 and Alaska. Jane was a beautiful, talented native woman who was an inspiration to the local residents and a terrific role model for the young girls in the village.

It was two fun-filled weeks for all of us. Teachers took turns cooking dinner for them and they cooked dinner for us once or twice. Almost every evening they had a jam session at one of the teacher's houses.

Dana made a tape for me of his Irish songs.

The parents and the villagers looked forward to the day of the performance with much excitement and enthusiasm. The gym was decorated to look like a theater and was filled to capacity. The performance was amazing. Many of the students were gifted and Dana and Jane seemed to bring their talents to life. There was a reception afterward with cookies and punch for everyone.

Somehow Dana got the ingredients for Black Russians and there was a private after cast party for the teachers. They were such a ray of sunshine in the dark, cold days of winter. We never wanted them to leave, so this was a bittersweet day for all of us. We didn't know if we would see them again. Although artists did come every year, we were not guaranteed to have the same ones.

Village Life: Food

There was an abundance of salmon and pike in the Kuskokwim River. The men did most of the fishing and the women cleaned, cut up, and prepared it for drying. They had racks where they hung the salmon fillets to dry during the summer months. Dry fish dipped in seal oil was a staple at their table. Almost all the families had a fish camp during the summer where they fished and prepared their catch for winter.

I was visiting Marian one afternoon and she was cutting up fish. She cut off the heads, cut out

Native women ice fishing with their children.

the eggs, and put them in a bucket. She then put the rest in another bucket. I thought she was throwing the heads and eggs away and going to freeze or cook the fish that she threw in the bucket. I had never eaten pike before so I asked if I could have one to cook for our dinner. She didn't answer me so I just let it go. Later I was told that I had embarrassed her by asking for dog food.

The heads and eggs were to be made into stink head. Stink head was a delicacy. The fish heads and eggs were buried down by the perma-frost with some grass on top. After it had aged and fermented they dug it up and ate it. I heard that if you could get it past your nose, it was delicious with lots of protein. I never managed to get it past my nose!!

A huge boatload of fresh seal came into the village one day and they were, I assumed, sold to the villagers. I saw wheelbarrows full of dead seals being pushed through the village. The blubber from the seal was cut into chunks and put into gallon jars. Over time the oil would liquefy. This was a staple in most homes to dunk your dry fish or fry bread into. Sometimes when I was walking down by the river a fishing boat would come in with a big catch of salmon and they would give me one.

Village Culture: Weddings

Some weddings were quiet simple ceremonies either at the church or the Justice of the Peace in Bethel. Martha's wedding was a classic. She wanted a traditional white gown, attendants, fresh flowers—the works. She had hired a minister to fly in, ordered flowers, bought a beautiful white wedding gown, decorated a hall, and had enough food prepared to feed the entire village and visiting guests. The morning of the wedding the minister called and explained that he was unable to fly into Akiak because of a storm. Not to be deterred, all the food was prepared so they went ahead with the reception as planned. The food was set out banquet style. I couldn't believe some of the guests brought containers and filled them to take home.

My first reaction was, "This is not right. They should at least wait until everyone has been served." Again I was faced with a different culture. They were taking some of the celebration home to elders or children who were not able to attend. I was learning that although our cultures were different, theirs was not wrong. In many ways it was a kind and caring tradition.

The next day the minister arrived and the wedding went as planned. The bride was beautiful in her white wedding dress. Snow covered the ground and it was very cold. Martha and her attendants waited in the arctic porch, without coats, for the recorded music to play the "Wedding March." The small church was filled with people dressed for the weather because it was not heated. Children were running up and down the aisles, babies were crying, and then the bride entered and all was quiet for a minute.

The ceremony took about 10 minutes and then the wedding party walked down the aisle, out of the church and into a sled pulled by a snow machine. About a hundred feet from the reception hall, the sled hit a bump and tipped over throwing the bride into the snow. I think at this point I would have been crying, but not Martha. They were all laughing, picking each other up and brushing off the snow.

Carlton (the school's principal) and his fiancé Lucy's wedding was also a challenge. They were married in her home village of Akiachak in the spring. Lucy and Carlton had met at a basketball game. She also had a traditional white wedding gown, bridesmaids, suits, flowers, and a lovely reception in her parent's home.

Because it was spring, the ground was muddy from the winter thaw. Although they all wore mud boots to and from the church, she did not escape without a few mud stains on her lovely wedding dress. There were always many small children running and laughing during the services. The Eskimo people loved their children, and didn't really believe in restricting them.

When Carlton brought his new wife Lucy back to the village, Helen asked her to babysit her children. After a few months of babysitting Lucy confided in me that she didn't want to babysit anymore. She was pregnant and sometimes fell asleep holding the baby. I told her to tell Helen that she was having problems and that maybe she could find someone else. Lucy said, "Then she will think I am lazy like you."

Steam Houses

Because there wasn't running water in most of the village, the steam houses were used for bathing. Each extended family had a steam house. Bob and Bill resurrected an old abandoned steam house and they used it a few times. After getting the fire very hot they put water on the hot rocks. It was so hot and steamy that the one time I tried it I couldn't breathe. Bob told me to wet a washcloth with cold water and put it over my face. I tried that, but hated the steam house. I put on my parka and ran outside and made snow angels in the snow to cool off. I would not have survived if I had been born an Eskimo.

As an experiment, Carlton opened the showers to the public one night a week. This didn't turn out well. Someone on staff had to be available to open and close the school, it was difficult to get the people out of the showers at a reasonable time and the toilets were always plugged and overflowing. Everything was a mess.

Summer 1982

I was always so happy to turn the calendar to the month of May. This meant the school year was coming to an end and we would soon be flying home for the summer.

This summer our plane landed at the Eugene airport. After a warm welcome from my boys, our first stop was at Dairy Queen for a peanut buster parfait. This continued to be a priority after nine months of dreaming about good ice cream.

Coming home from Alaska though found our oldest son Jeff's marriage in trouble. His wife, Susan, had moved out with Joshua. Jeff had custody of Josh most of the summer and we loved having him with us. Joshua was an adorable little guy, a bit hyper, but almost too smart for his own good. He had a loving personality with hugs and kisses for everyone. He knew even at the tender age of three that we were leaving at the end of the summer. This made it even harder for us to say goodbye. When we had to say goodbye he wouldn't give us hugs. He just turned away and said he didn't like us anymore.

Our 25th wedding anniversary was coming up in October so our children planned an early anniversary party for us at the Redland, Oregon Grange Hall. It was a sweet gesture and although I don't react well to surprises, I had a wonderful time despite my misgivings. We had a great visit with family and old friends. We even watched a video of our wedding 25 years ago.

Our daughter Mindy now had an adorable baby boy, Brendan and we got home for the summer almost in time for his first birthday. Tom, our son-in-law, was graduating from the University of Oregon with a teaching degree. Because staff was constantly changing in Akiak, there was an opening for an elementary teacher for the next school year. Somehow, we managed to talk Tom into applying for that teaching position and he found out in July that he had been hired to teach the elementary grades. The rest of the summer became one filled with anticipation, shopping, and planning.

My life in the village was getting better and better. Having my daughter and her family close was a dream come true. We bought a "cozy coup" car for Brendan that summer and took it with us to the village. It turned out to be the best thing ever. It was a peddle car on the trails and a sled in the snow. The village boys loved to push him or pull him around in his miniature car.

Again, August came way too fast and time to say goodbye to our summer vacation. However, it was easier going back to Alaska now that our daughter would be there too, and our three sons were living in our family home.

Year Three (Akiak)

Flying into Akiak this year was a whole new experience, seeing the village through my daughter's eyes.

Debbie had taken part of the year off to get treatment for an eating disorder, and her sister, Maurine, came from New England and filled in for her. Although we missed Debbie, Maurine was a delightful addition to the staff.

The first week back in the village I was showing Mindy and Brendan around and we took a short cut through some tall dried grass. As I was walking along with Brendan in my arms I fell into an abandoned honey bucket hole that was not covered. As I started to fall I threw Brendan onto solid ground. Luckily, there were old honey buckets and other garbage down in the hole so I didn't sink so far that I couldn't crawl out. School was in session so I could go to the shower and get cleaned up and dispose of my ruined shoes without too many spectators—another of my many mishaps with honey buckets.

Our daughter Mindy and her family were like light in an otherwise dark, dreary winter. Mindy did some subbing and coached the girls' volleyball and basketball teams. She also coached the cheerleaders.

Mindy and her Dad in Akiak.

Being young and energetic, she was an asset in many ways and a role model for many of the young girls. It was Tom's first year as a teacher and I am sure not easy for him to jump right into a culture so different than he was used to. However, he did a magnificent job teaching and coached some sports as well.

Brendan, in his feet-covered pajamas, was a frequent visitor to our house. One of his favorite games was playing stories that his papa (Bob) read to him. He called Bob, Foxy Loxy and I think he was Chicken Little. Sometimes I was included in the game and was Turkey Lurky or Lucy Goosey. He loved "He Man" and entertained us with his sword, raising it over his head and saying "By the power of Greyskull . . . He Man!" or putting on his top hat, saying, "adies and gentlemen!" He didn't say his els.

One day I fell on my way home from the store with a dozen eggs. I told Brendan, "I'm glad I didn't break my eggs," This made Brendan laugh, "You talk like me," he said. He thought I was saying I didn't break my legs. Falling happened a lot because there were no cleared walkways and lots of slippery surfaces. Funny how when you fall the first thing you do is look around to make sure no one saw you being clumsy.

October 26th was our 25th wedding anniversary. Bob was scheduled to attend a workshop in Anchorage the weekend of our anniversary. Although we already had an early celebration, it didn't seem right to be separated on this big occasion. The other teachers bought me an airline ticket so I could go with Bob. I found out nothing is easy in the bush. When we got to the airport in Bethel they said the plane was overbooked and I would have to fly standby. Of course we packed both our things in one suitcase. There was a tense 30 or 40 minutes waiting to see if I could get on the flight or if I had to spend a night in Bethel and go back to the village. After I did get to board, the passengers on the plane were even kind enough to move so that I could sit with my husband. We ended up having a nice weekend with dinner and a movie.

At the Halloween party at school, Bob dressed like a witch, warts and all. Brendan cried when he heard his papa's voice coming out of the witch's mouth. He thought the witch had eaten his papa. So later, when Bob played Santa at the Christmas party, he didn't talk. He just said "ho ho-ho" and handed out candy.

Our youngest child, Aaron, came to visit on his Christmas vacation. He wore cowboy boots and a light jacket. When he got off the charter plane it was so cold my ballpoint pen wouldn't even write, and here was my son dressed for weather in Oregon. I had to write the check for his airfare with a pencil. While he was visiting he could wear Bob's boots and parka so he didn't freeze to death. We thoroughly enjoyed showing him around the village, ice fishing, walking across the frozen river, snow machine riding, and introducing him to our life in Alaska. The young girls in the village were quite taken with Aaron.

Village Culture: Babysitting

One of the high school girls from my home economics class was absent from school for several days. The reason, as I later found out, was she was the only one home to babysit her year-and-a-half-old nephew. Her mother and the baby's mother were in Anchorage supposedly on a spree. I volunteered to watch the baby for her so she could go to her morning classes. This created some rumblings about how I had declined to baby sit for some and then offered to watch someone else's child.

I never really understood all their customs. Apparently, the visiting teacher from Bethel who spent a week in our village working with some of the adults to get their GED, heard this. He told me I had insulted Helen by not watching her children. He said the Eskimo people cherished their children and it was a compliment that she thought of me like a sister and trusted me to care for her children. Maybe I should have apologized to Helen, but so much time had passed by then that I just let it go.

Medical Adventure

I don't remember the event, but one day we were all outside watching something and a three wheeler hit little Brendan and he suffered a concussion, lots of bruises, and multiple cuts. We immediately got a plane to take us to Bethel to the hospital to treat him. Mindy carried him and I rode along. When we arrived at the hospital they said he wasn't unconscious or bleeding so they wouldn't do anything for him. We were told to take him to the family clinic. Another taxi ride to the family clinic and no one was there. The office was locked up and closed. Here we were in freezing weather with a scared little boy, his worried mom and terrified grandma, and no one to help us.

We were frantic and our only recourse was to knock on doors and find out how to contact the person that manned the family clinic. After waiting in the cold for several hours a doctor finally came, checked Brendan out, and treated his injuries. Because he was such a good patient the doctor gave him a black, plastic spider. Brendan hated it and it made him feel worse. Probably not something to make a two-year old feel good, especially if they are afraid of spiders.

A few weeks later Brendan had a big purple bulge appear under his upper eye lid. This entailed another trip to Bethel. My Oregon neighbor Marvin had sent me a big purple silk flower and, of course, Brendan accused that flower of causing his problem, which he called the "big purple." His condition cleared up in a few days and he was okay, but he never forgot about that "big purple," so I had to get rid of the flower.

Brendan was such an adorable little boy. He entertained himself by reading books sitting in his little rocking chair that his papa made for him. Bob also made him a "hurky" high chair. All the villagers were impressed with his high chair and someone bought it when we left the village. I wish we could have taken it with us. It was an heirloom. Sometimes when Brendan and I were making cookies or playing a game and someone knocked on the door to visit, Brendan would say,

"You can't come in now, this is my special time with grandma."

When the river is frozen cars can be driven between Bethel and some of the villages. Instead of chartering a flight you could hire a river taxi. An African American river taxi driver was spending some time at our house waiting for the weather to change so he could go back to Bethel. Brendan was also at our house visiting and the man showed him a trick with his fingers. Brendan was fascinated by his trick and the man said, "Try it. You can do it." Brendan replied, "No, I can't, I don't have dirty hands." This made the taxi driver laugh.

My Home Economics Class

This year, my home economics class decided to create a restaurant. The first dinner was an Italian meal. The students planned the menu: salad, spaghetti, French bread, and a dessert. They practiced making this meal until they were comfortable with it. They set a date when the restaurant would be open and sold tickets ahead of the event. They could only accommodate 20 in their restaurant and had no trouble selling all the tickets. They set up tables and chairs in a section of the gym and added candles, silk flowers, and soft music. They wore aprons made in the sewing class, seated their guests, and served the meal. They were also responsible for cleaning up afterward. It was a great success.

Every month they prepared a different ethnic meal and had the restaurant open for one evening. The students were allowed to accept and keep tips from the restaurant. The money from the bake sales and restaurants was put into a fund for the class to go on field trips. Our big field trip was to Bethel to eat dinner at a real restaurant! The biggest expense of going anywhere was the chartered plane and taxi fares.

Adam, one of the student's father, had served as a cook in the military, and he gave us some of his favorite Chinese recipes, including how to make fortune cookies. Adam was an interesting man. He tried to make his surroundings more like his experiences in the lower 48 states. On Thanksgiving he made a traditional turkey dinner instead of the customary fish or wild meat dinner. He invited the Gussocks to share his Thanksgiving Day meal. The Kawagley family, Adam and Catherine, had four beautiful daughters and finally on their fifth try they were blessed with a son.

I was invited to give a presentation about my class's bakery and restaurant events at a home economics conference in Anchorage. I was so nervous. What was I doing talking to a group of real teachers? Surprisingly, it all went better than I had expected and I ended up having a good time. Traveling alone and staying at the hotel by myself was another stressful moment. As luck would have it, Jerry and Helen were in Anchorage at the same time. They saved my life by coming over to the hotel every evening and taking me out to dinner, and one night we went to a disco. I encountered a small problem the first night I was there. When I went to get into Jerry's car a drunk or homeless man tried to get into the car with me. After that, Jerry and Helen walked me back to my room.

As the close of our third year approached there was no discussion about whether we would be returning the next fall. I guess there was no question that because Mindy and Tom were coming back, we would also. Even though life was getting better in the village, I still counted the days until school would be over, and we would have three months in Oregon.

Summer 1983

Bob still had his commercial fishing boat, the "Phyllis" and did some salmon fishing at the coast this summer. Bill visited with us in June and we took him to see Crater Lake. It was unbelievable. There were mounds of snow everywhere and it was so foggy you could not see the lake. We ended up buying a postcard and Aaron took a picture of Bill standing by the railing of the lake and he photoshopped a picture that was almost believable of the lake behind him.

My mother was beginning to show signs of Alheimers so we spent more time with her. There was a Weigel (my Mother's maiden name) family reunion every July and our Bolkan family picnic at Barton Park. Our traditional "Jump off the Rock" contest at Fall Creek for Mindy's birthday on August 13th was the highlight of every summer. We had a picnic by the swimming hole and the brave tried a new and original jump from this 15-foot rock into the swimming hole. The "chickens" were the judges. I fell into this category, and rated the jumpers from 1 to 10. The winner was awarded with a rock trophy and had to do the "Poppy Dance" with Mindy.

Again, too soon it was time to ship supplies, give the boys last minute instructions about the house, and say our goodbyes until the Christmas holidays.

Fourth Year (Akiak)

Mindy was pregnant with her second child the fourth year and we made a trip to Bethel to see her doctor. Trips were never predictable or easy. Because it was too foggy for us to land in Bethel, we landed in Nunapitchuk and took a river taxi to Bethel. She got there in time for her appointment, but the fog didn't lift and the plane couldn't fly when it was time for us to go home. Not wanting to spend the night in the local hotel, we waited around the marketplace until we heard that there was a river taxi going to Akiak later that evening. They had room for us for a price.

I had never driven on the frozen river in a car before and was frantic every time the driver stopped and idled in one spot, certain the heat from the exhaust would melt the ice and we would fall through it into the river. It was impossible to see where we were going. The fog was so dense against the snow and ice on the ground, I don't know how the taxi driver could tell where he was going. Everything was white.

Some places in the river never freeze completely, so if you drive there you can break through. I can still feel the anxiety when I think about that taxi ride. All I could think of was, I should have stayed in Bethel and not risked my daughter's and little grandson's lives on this crazy adventure. With the help of our guardian angel, and many Hail Marys, we arrived home safely.

Back at the village, everything was changing and our close-knit group of teachers was breaking up. Debbie and Bill got married and transferred to another village. Kathy also got a transfer. Eventually, all three of them accepted teaching jobs in Juneau and made their home in the beautiful capital of Alaska. We spent a week with them on our way home after a school year and fell in love with Juneau. The beautiful scenery, glaciers, boat rides, and hiking trails, but most of all the precious time spent with wonderful friends.

A Head Start program was started in Akiak and a teaching couple was hired to live and manage the program in the old BIA building.

This couple brought their young daughter with them to the village. Several of their older children had remained in their hometown. This little girl had blonde hair like Brendan. Before she came, he thought something was wrong with him. One day he asked, "Why do I have ugly hair?" My blue-eyed, blonde grandson was teased because he was different. Some adults even asked if he was blind because his eyes were so blue. Apparently, the villagers were as confused about my culture as I was about theirs.

On Tom's 30th birthday we were having a little party at the school and the school phone rang. The call was for the Head Start couple. They received the nightmare call that every parent dreads. One of their children was in an accident and was taken to the morgue. They didn't even know which child it was until the next morning. Their teenage daughter lost control of her car on an icy road. No one really recovers from losing a child. They were never the same after they came back to the village and finished out the school year.

The village was abuzz with excitement. A grant made it possible for some of the residents to get prefab housing. These buildings were three- and four-bedroom houses, complete with inside plumbing. No more honey buckets! House parts and material arrived by barge and construction crews invaded the village.

They were reasonably nice homes, but it wasn't long before the plumbing was plugged up, faucets were leaking, and they had to revert back to using honey buckets. There was no one to contact for repair services and the Yup'iks had no training on maintenance when there was a problem.

In November, an Eskimo family that was going to spend the winter in Dillingham asked us if we would rent their home and take care of it until May when they returned. We agreed. The house was one big room with partitions for the bedroom and bathroom. Mindy made shades for the bare windows and I packed their personal belongings into boxes and stored them. They left with just clothes and some personal items. A VCR was left in the house that we could use while they were gone. Friends and our kids sent us movie tapes so we were able to watch the television miniseries "The Thorn Birds" as well as a number of good movies. We mailed them the rent each month and everything went well until April when they came home early. We offered to move our things into the school gym for the remainder of the school year, but they wanted us to pay rent for May and they would live with relatives in the village until we left for the summer.

A short time after they returned the husband asked Bob for money. Unaware that the money was to buy liquor, Bob lent him $40. A few days later he needed another $40. Bob told him he couldn't afford to give him any more money. That night around 10 o'clock he was at our door, drunk. Because it was his house he came right in and explained he now needed $80.

I was already in bed. Bob was trying to calm him down and get him to leave. Instead, he sat down and talked for hours, occasionally saying obnoxious things about me. At around 12:30 a.m. I mentioned from the bedroom that Bob needed to get some sleep so he could teach the next day. I guess that angered him and made him even more belligerent. Sometime before 4:00 in the morning he took down one of his guns that he left hanging on a gun rack. He said something like, "I could shoot you now." It may have only been a threat to get the money, but we will never know. When he found that we had unloaded all the guns in the house, he checked all the drawers and climbed up on the counters and looked on top of the cupboards to find some bullets. When he didn't find any ammo he accepted a cup of coffee and then left.

I am not sure what Bob felt at that moment when he said, "I could shoot you right now." I know I was shaking with fear and wishing I had a loaded gun to protect us. I probably couldn't have shot him, but at least I could have chased him out of the house. This was one of many times I regretted ever coming to Alaska. Renting from the Eskimos was not a good idea for any of us.

The next day, I packed up and moved out. I refused to spend another night in that house not knowing if or when he would be back with ammo in his gun. We moved our stuff into the school gym and slept at Mindy's house. It was only a few weeks before school was out and we would be safe back home in Oregon with our family.

After five years as principal in Akiak, Carlton Kuhns resigned and took a job in Bethel. He now had a wife and two little girls. Living in Bethel would be easier for them, but we really missed having them in the village. Carlton had been such a comfort and support for us during our first years in village life. He was wise beyond his years in his relationships and dealings with both cultures. There was one advantage for us in their move. We now had a contact in Bethel and their house had indoor plumbing.

Summer 1985

Baby Treg was born on July 26ᵗʰ, a beautiful healthy little brother for Brendan. Much of our summer revolved around this new addition to our family. We enjoyed many of the same picnics and reunions, plus we added the Enchanted Forest near Salem to our traditional outings. Brendan and Joshua were now old enough to enjoy the amusement park.

Mindy stayed in Oregon with Brendan and the baby until he was a little bigger. Marian McLaughlin, Mindy's mother-in-law, graciously agreed to fly with Mindy and the boys to Akiak in October. We loved spending time with her and showing her around the village. It was very hard to raise small children so far from medical care and no modern conveniences. By now the school had a telephone and we were allowed to use it for emergencies and sometimes on weekends if we paid for time and charges.

When Bob and I returned in August, we moved into one of the teacher houses across from the school. I avoided David, the man who had threatened us, but eventually I ran into him at a basketball game and he said, "I'm going to pay you back." I wasn't sure what that meant. Of course, he never repaid the loan, but I was glad to never see him again.

We loved having our daughter and her family living so close and being able to be a part of my grandson's lives. It was such a special time. We did many things together. Mindy was and still is very talented and crafty. We made hooked rugs from old clothes and she made beautiful quilts with appliqué depicting Eskimo art. We also experimented with recipes and came up with 50 ways to cook ptarmigan. I had a pasta maker and Brendan and I made pasta, baked cookies, and played together. He found part of a bike. It was just a big, black wheel with handlebars. He pulled it around on the boardwalks calling it his "Black Wheel." I know it was hard for them working and raising two small boys with very little modern conveniences. Because disposable diapers weren't available, Mindy had to use cloth diapers. Luckily, we lived just feet away from the school so she could do laundry there. It was a taste of life 40 years before when I was a young child growing up without modern conveniences.

Our new principal was Robert Day from Idaho. Bob met the Days, Robert and his wife Billie, at the air strip with the school tractor and a sled to transport all their luggage and their cat, Sylvester, to their new lodgings. Sylvester was a huge black and white tom cat. They moved into the house that had been Bob's and my first teacher house, the one with the built in kitchen sink. Because of the many dogs and other wild animals they didn't feel comfortable letting Sylvester outside. They put a trap door in the arctic porch with steps so their cat could have some time to hunt and sort of be outside. It was like he had his own apartment in the basement.

Robert and Billie Day.

Robert and Billie were both retired and looking forward to an adventure in Alaska. Robert had been a school teacher, principal, and administrator. Billie had also led a very interesting life. She sold real estate and insurance, had her own restaurant in Idaho, was a horse jockey, and a gold miner, to name but a few of her adventures. They were an instant fit with the other teachers. From the beginning it seemed like I had known them forever and they became very dear friends. Robert Day was an excellent principal with many years of experience. His calm, easygoing demeanor fostered loyalty and trust. Billie was enthusiastic and outgoing with a great sense of humor. I was in awe of her ability to turn a virtual stranger into a friend almost immediately. She was also an excellent cook and we shared many good meals and card games together. Billie always had chocolate. When she baked, the smell of her goodies led you straight to her house.

In addition to our new principal, three new teachers were added to our ever-changing staff: Terry and Boyce, both single young men, and Diana, a beautiful, young native woman.

Robert Day had a hard time dealing with the feeds. Fish was not his favorite food to begin with. However, because he was the school principal he felt compelled to attend these affairs. Things were not always the most sanitary at the houses hosting the feeds either. At one house they had set a big pot of fish soup on the floor to make room for another pot on the stove. A little barefoot girl stepped into the pot of soup. She wasn't burned, so the mother simply wiped her legs off and continued to serve the soup. As I mentioned before, the soup contained the fish heads and eyeballs, for which the Eskimo children often fought over. On the way home from the feed Robert lost his dinner on the trail.

This year, a big yellow tom cat was observed in the village, and there was a lot of talk about what to do with him. He was friendly and hungry and followed some of the children. His ears and paws were frostbitten. The children were afraid of him, and if I had not taken him in, one of the parents would have shot him. Being a cat lover, I lured him into my house with warm milk. He could only drink small amounts and refused any solid food for several days. I made a litter box and he was easily trained.

We never found out where he came from or how he got to our village. Terry, one of the teachers, helped me shave his belly and cut out all the mats in his fur. After a couple weeks he was eating solid food and table scraps, gaining weight, and walking normally on his healed paws. The tips of his ears were badly frostbitten and he eventually lost both tips. The kids grew to like him and always asked, "Is yours cat here?" In fact, the only reason many of them came to visit after that was to pet the cat. I didn't have to choose a name for him. He simply became known as "Yours Cat."

We didn't go home for the Christmas holidays this year. Some winters it was too hard to travel in and out of the village because there was only a short window of time when it was daylight, and if the weather was bad the plane couldn't even fly at all. Robert and Billy Day had agreed to spend some of the holidays taking care of a friend's bed and breakfast in Bethel. They didn't have much business during that time and Bob and I spent some time at the bed and breakfast with Robert and Billie. I remember playing pinochle for hours with them.

The second part of the year that

Yours Cat.

the Days were in Akiak, the village corporation decided to raise the teacher's rent from $600 a month to almost double. Robert found a vacant cabin in the village that was used to fix snow machines and butcher wild game. They could rent this shack for around $500 a month. It took Billie and I nearly a week to scrub and disinfect that house, which unfortunately, still had an odor. All the drawers in the kitchen had grease and junk in them. The floor smelled like rotten game. It was a mess. There was an oil heater with an oil drum outside the building, and an old fashioned wood range to cook and heat water.

Billie had a way with making any situation work and she turned that stinky cabin into a warm and cozy nest. One night in the middle of winter when it was about 40 degrees below zero, they woke up to the sound of their diet Pepsi popping. The heat had gone off and it was freezing in their house. They put on their warmest clothes and all the blankets they had until daylight. Then, they went to the school and warmed up. Someone had deliberately shut off the oil from the outside. This could have been a serious health hazard. Later that day the male teachers got the heater working and notified the local police so they could monitor the area. We never found out who the culprits were, but assumed it was some angry students.

The villagers voted to go Yup'ik Nation and have their own schools. They wanted to have more control over the content taught and to hire locals to teach the native crafts and preserve their culture. Bob was asked to stay with the school but declined. All the staff requested transfers to other villages. Bob and Billie transferred to the coastal village of Nunapitchuk. Mindy and Tom moved to North Pole where Tom got a teaching position at the high school. North Pole is basically a suburb of Fairbanks and is a town much like you'd find in the lower 48. They needed to get a place on the road system. It was too hard to get medical care in the bush, and not practical with two small children. Terry, Bob, and I accepted a transfer to Atmautluak, a village about 100 miles west of Akiak.

Leaving Akiak

The thought may have entered my mind about going home instead of accepting the transfer, but it was not the best choice for us at that time. Neither of us had a job in Oregon. The timber economy back home was tanking. We still had children in college. Teacher pay in Alaska was double what Bob could get in Oregon and we had a good retirement system in place, and excellent life and medical insurance that was paid by the school district. Bob loved the outdoor hunting and fishing, plus we had made lifelong friends and the living conditions had improved greatly. I was looking forward to a new adventure in another village.

Before going home to Oregon for the summer we packed up everything we would be taking to the new village and stored the boxes at the school. Then we packed the things that we would be taking home for the summer. When summer came we gave a little girl in the village a supply of cat food and she took care of Yours Cat until we came back in August to move to our new village. We had our reservations to fly home to Oregon and were prepared to close up the house. When the day to leave finally arrived a ferocious wind storm came up and planes couldn't fly.

Brendan was so looking forward to going to "the place where you don't wear coats." He sat on our kitchen table looking out the window, holding my rosary and saying, "Please God, stop the wind!" With everything already packed, staying longer would entail a lot of extra work and nothing to eat. Late in the afternoon the mail plane flew in and the pilot said he could fly us to Bethel, but we would have to leave some of our luggage. Jerry and Helen were at the airstrip with us and said they would ship our luggage later.

Taking off from the air strip the wind caused the plane to drift toward the trees. We cleared them by inches. We came so close we could have reached out of the window and touched the branches. The whole ride to Bethel was bumpy and by far the scariest plane ride I had ever encountered. In my terror I said, "This isn't the day I wanted to die." Mindy's look of dismay brought me back to reality. I was upsetting the children.

Year 6, A New Village (Atmautluak)

Flying back to Akiak for the last time felt in many ways like the first time. This was just one leg of our journey to a new community. Terry moved a lot of our things by boat and one of the items was Yours Cat in a cage. Afraid of the water and having to endure hours on the river with Terry, Yours Cat never forgave him. Every time Terry came to our house after that he would pee on his parka.

Atmautluak was another new experience. We had a real two-bedroom house, a bathroom with a built-in chemical toilet and shower, a living and dining room, plus a kitchen with a range, refrigerator, and sink with running water. We had actual cupboards and closets. A large water tank in the bathroom held enough water to last a couple weeks. It had an opening on the outside of the house where we could use the school's water hose to fill our tank when it ran out.

The big problem with this, however, was that during the summer a bird had gotten into the water tank. Unaware that birds were in there, we filled the tank and I even drank some of the water. We didn't know what had happened until I took a shower and feathers came out of the spout. It was literally a bird bath. We drained the tank and Bob climbed down in the tank to

Our house in Atmautluak, with the stinky, abandoned chest freezer out front.

Atmautluak.

scrub it with Clorox. Mindy had flown with us to the village. Even with her help we had a hard time getting Bob out when the fumes got so bad he couldn't breathe. He coughed for a long time after that. Not a great idea to put Clorox and Bob in the same tank. What were we thinking? This could have been a disaster.

We had a large arctic porch. In our front yard stood an old chest freezer that had been removed from the arctic porch before we arrived. The tenants before us had left the freezer full of meat and fish hoping to transfer them to their new home at the end of summer. The generator was off part of the summer and everything spoiled. The rotten fluid had permeated the floor boards in the porch. Although it had been scrubbed many times with pine cleaner and every kind of disinfectant and deodorizer, every time I entered the porch the smell was overpowering. Finally, I put some rugs over it and it helped a little. We were able to get a new chest freezer that was great for storing our salmon and wild birds.

Unlike Akiak, Atmautluak had no trees and the ground was tundra. Although they had built boardwalks to and from all the houses, stepping off the boardwalk resulted in sinking into muck. I can't count how many times I lost my boot in the muck and Bob had to retrieve it. The only time you could walk on the ground was when it was frozen. The village is very flat with a view of mountains in the horizon. Atmautluak had two churches, the Moravian church at one end of the village and the Russian Orthodox Church at the other end.

I went to one service at the Russian Orthodox Church. The women sat or stood on one side and the men on the other. It was totally different than the Catholic church services. When they entered the church they kissed an icon. I'm not sure what the significance of separating the men from the women was. We stood the whole time. I also went to their Slovak celebration after the Christmas holiday. It was one way of meeting all the villagers and participating in their celebration.

I didn't have a class of my own at this school, but I did sub for teachers. The first two months of the school year I subbed for the first grade teacher Clair, who was on sick leave after having a baby. Every Friday, the staff made breakfast for the students; pancakes, scrambled eggs, bacon, the whole works. Sometimes I helped. With music and continuous joking going on in the background, cooking breakfast was always fun!

The principal, Ray, and his wife Marilyn both taught at the high school. Bob, Cliff, Terry, Jim, and Clair were the other teachers. The three guys were all single so they spent a lot of time at our house. There was a weekly poker game and a party whenever we wanted to celebrate, which was usually for no reason, but happened often.

Ray had his own private plane in the village and we flew with him several times. One trip to Dillingham was especially interesting and fun. It was not work related. On Mother's Day weekend we flew

Cliff, Jim, Bob, Olinka, and Terry.

A typical Alaskan bush plane, not my favorite mode of transportation.

to Dillingham to meet his parents and so he could spend time with his mother. We saw the town, had a fun meal at a restaurant, and played some games at his house. A little ray of civilization was always appreciated. Ray gave all the women a red rose for Mother's Day.

Ray's plane had floats so that we could land and take off on the river, which was an exciting experience for me, especially the time we had too many fish and we were too heavy to get up off the ground high enough to clear the trees. As usual, I panicked. We had to lighten our load. I'm sure they would have liked to have left me there, but instead they left some of the fish behind.

Jim was a first year teacher in Alaska and taught the English classes. Before coming to Alaska he lived in Ashland, Oregon. One of his daughters, Rachel, spent a week with us in the village. We always enjoyed his visits.

Olinka and I would usually play cribbage on the nights the guys played poker. Olinka was one of the teacher aides at the school. She was a delightful young single mother with a five-year-old daughter, whose name was Paula. The kids in Atmautluak were curious about our cat at first, but grew to love him, especially Paula. Yours Cat would often wander into the classroom during school and curl up and sleep in a corner. There was one problem with our pet cat. We learned very early not to leave our suitcases out where he could see them. Somehow he knew we were going away and he would pee in the suitcase.

We only had Yours Cat in Atmautluak for one year. Before we left for the summer Paula had offered to feed him during our absence. When we returned in August we were told that Yours Cat had been shot by someone in the village. They accused him of going into their arctic porches and stealing fish. I had tried to feed him salmon, but he would never eat it. The thing that bothered me the most was the children's reaction. They seemed to delight in the fact that the cat had been shot and they wanted to tell me all the gory details.

It was hard for me to understand killing a sweet little cat. I came to understand this was another area where our customs clashed. Children here were raised to be hunters and fishermen. Animals were only used for work, food, or hides. Cats didn't fit into any of those categories, and pets were not something they were used to.

During our second year in Atmoutlauk there was another romance blooming. Terry asked Bob to be his best man, and Terry and Olinka were married by the Justice of the Peace in Bethel. Although Olinka had done a great job as a single mom in the bush, we were very happy that the two of them got together and had a ready-made family.

Bob loved the outdoor life, hunting and fishing, and although the natives were allowed to shoot swans, that was one thing Bob would not kill. We did eat swan when some of the villagers prepared it. Once I was given a swan by a native family. Getting all the feathers off and cleaning it was difficult. I cooked it, but was not impressed. Some of the natives freeze the bird with feathers on to keep it from getting freezer burn. I couldn't imagine thawing out a bird and then trying to dress it.

Cliff taught the shop classes at the high school. He also had a small private plane and pilot's license. He took me to Bethel to get groceries one afternoon when I was desperate for fresh fruits and veggies. By the time we had our purchases and started our flight back to the village, it was getting dark. Everything takes longer than you anticipate. Atmautluak did not have lights on the runway so you could only land during the daylight hours. In winter there was only a five-hour window of daylight. As we neared our destination, Cliff said, "I have to land on the river." At first I thought he was kidding me. On the flight to Bethel he had been doing some flips and turns to scare me. Little did he know, I was scared to fly with him even without his maneuvers. Although we landed safely, that was the only time I flew with him to get groceries.

Bob coached the wrestling team and he traveled with the team on away matches. Usually I went along. We would pack our things out to the airstrip and wait for our plane to land. It was always cold. To entertain themselves while waiting, the kids had spitting contests. Sometimes the spit would freeze before it hit the ground. Because there was only four to five hours of daylight, flying to the school for a match took two days. This meant we had to sleep over in the gym in sleeping bags. The host school usually provided the evening meal. Breakfast was the responsibility of the visiting school's coach. They had supplies in the kitchen, but we had to prepare it for our team.

During one trip to Dillingham we were snowed in for most of the week. I loved Dillingham before the bad weather came. It reminded me of a small coastal town in Oregon. The ships came in and brought fresh fruits and vegetables once a week. It was almost like an island. One side was calm and the other side had more severe weather. Flying there was like looking over vast fields of meringue.

Lost in a Blizzard

Bob took his wrestlers to a nearby village by snow machine for a match. He pulled the sled filled with their gear and the team members rode their own snow machines. A terrible blizzard (whiteout) came up on their way home. When the storm hit and Bob didn't return with the boys we were all panicking. I spent most of the time at the principal's house awaiting a break in the storm and praying. The principal's son was one of the wrestlers. I think it was a couple days, but it may have been just one night before we heard the sound of snow machines coming into the village.

Bob and his wrestling team in Atmautluak.

All were safe and healthy. At the first sign that they had lost the trail, Bob stopped the boys, put up a tent and got them all inside. They were not even allowed to go out to pee. A couple of the boys wanted to go on home. They said they were sure of the direction of the village. Good thing Bob didn't listen to them because they were completely turned around and they would have gotten themselves lost and died. Bob was knighted village Hero when he brought those kids home safe and he had gained their love and respect—imagine that, a gussock who knew what he was doing!

During the two years we were in Atmautluak, I was called for grand jury duty for six months. I had to fly to Bethel every other week for usually a one-day session. They paid for my airfare and lunch. If we didn't finish by 5:00 p.m. and had to spend the night they would pay for one night at the local hotel. The cases were almost all drug or alcohol related. It was interesting to hear the accused's version of the incident and make a decision about whether it should go to trial or not. We never saw the victims, only read their reports. The downside of this job was that it was during the fall and the hours of daylight were not long enough so I usually had to stay at least one night in Bethel. I didn't feel safe staying at the hotel because usually there were drunks hanging around, empty bottles, and not much security. Instead, I stayed with the Kellers, our old friends from Akiak. They were always gracious, and made me feel like part of the family.

In a small village school, the teachers are involved in all the kids' activities during and after school. Bob and I chaperoned the senior trip. All the seniors went to Seward with us to check out the vocational school there. Seward is located about 440 miles from Atmautluak along the Gulf of Alaska. We also visited nearby Anchorage and visited the college. Keeping these teenagers in line was not an easy task. We stayed in hotels and although they were told not to leave their hotel rooms without asking for permission, some of them snuck out. We also spent some time at a farm in Palmer. It was amazing to watch as the kids saw farm animals for the first time. They rode the horses and petted the bunnies and goats, but they were most fascinated by the chickens for some reason. They followed them around trying to take their picture.

The following summer we heard that one of the senior boys had died. They were playing a game that went wrong and he accidently hanged himself.

That summer, our youngest sons, Jason and Aaron, who had spent the winter working at a ski resort near Denver were driving home to Oregon and we planned a family trip to Reno. Jim, the English teacher in Atmautluak, who was spending the summer in his home town in Southern Oregon planned to go with us. Cliff, who was flying his plane to visit family in the states, was also meeting us in Reno. Our sons had car trouble on their way home to Oregon and were delayed so Cliff offered to fly them to Reno when he came.

We went ahead, picked up Jim and drove to Reno. The boys didn't arrive in Reno when they were supposed to, and I was having another attack of worry until Cliff called our hotel and left a message that the weather was bad and he couldn't cross the mountains safely. He had gotten a hotel room and a six pack of beer and they were waiting until the wind died down in Ashland. They made the flight without incident the next day. We ended up having a wonderful time with our sons and friends from Alaska. It was one big party. Cliff had so much fun drinking and playing blackjack one night that we found him the next morning at the same table where we left him the night before. He had a pile of chips in front of him and looked like he was about to fall asleep. We convinced him to take a break, get something to eat and maybe a nap.

Jeff, Mindy, and her friend Bev also met us, so all my kids were there. It turned out to be a fun mini vacation. The flashing lights and ringing bells of Reno made everything so exciting after so long in the quiet primitive environment of village life. At least it was fun for me and didn't involve camping or fishing. One of the things I missed so much was just getting in my car and going to the mall or out to lunch with friends.

Living in Atmautluak was harder for me. My daughter and her family were living in North Pole and I missed them all, especially my two young grandsons. We visited them at Christmas the second year they were in North Pole. I made the boys mukluks (hand-sewn hide and fur boots) for Christmas. Spending the holidays and watching Brendan and Treg on Christmas morning was a treat. We played in the snow, visited a couple of teachers we had taught with in another village, and because it was the first time we had been in North Pole, we went to Santa's Village. It was these little mini vacations at Christmas and summertime that made my life in Alaska bearable and provided me with warm memories.

The only other time I flew with Cliff was when Bob woke one night with chest pains and night sweats—all the symptoms of a heart attack. At daylight, Cliff offered to fly us to the Bethel hospital. The villages have health aides who call doctors in Bethel or Anchorage to get a diagnosis or medicine for the sick and injured. In emergencies a plane would be called to take the patient to the hospital. Cliff's offer was the quickest. Bob spent three days in the BIA hospital. His heart seemed to be okay. The pain went away with some antacids but his blood test showed a high white count, so the diagnosis was that Bob had pericarditis; inflammation around the heart. He was given a prescription for antibiotics and sent home. This was one of the many times Bob tried to quit smoking. For Bob, quitting was easy, he had done it a hundred times.

While Bob was in the hospital I stayed with Jerry and Helen Keller. They were great friends and opened their home to us whenever we had to spend a night in Bethel. They owned a van and drove me to and from the hospital and back and forth from the airport. They were so compassionate

Jerry and Helen Keller with two of their kids.

and helped keep me together while Bob was sick. They were our family away from home. We depended on each other and became good friends. After we moved home they continued to visit nearly every year on their travels to the lower 48 states.

We only spent two years in Atmautluak. There seemed to be some sort of political upheaval in the village and Bob and many of the other teachers asked to be transferred. That spring Bob got a transfer to Quinahauk, Jim transferred to the village of Eek, and Cliff got a transfer to Bethel High school.

When we got home that summer Bob got a check up with a cardiologist and there was no sign of his pericarditis so we thought he was ok. Pericarditis is a condition in which the sac-like covering around the heart (pericardium) becomes inflamed. Maybe it is better not to know some things—I'm glad I didn't know the way it all would end.

Late that summer we took a trip to Cabo San Lucas and rented a condo with my brother John and his wife Linda. It was a fun vacation until Linda became so ill we had to call the local doctor. We thought we were so careful not to drink the water, but we had eaten some popsicles from a street vender. I didn't get the stomach upset until on our way home. We were flying directly back to Alaska with a stopover in Portland to pick up our luggage. Needless to say it wasn't a very pleasant trip home, although we were able to sit in first-class close to the restroom. When we got to Bethel I was so glad we were going to spend the night at Carlton and Lucy's house—they had an indoor bathroom. My problem with honey buckets was still haunting me. Unfortunately, they had plumbing problems while we were there and we ended up having to use the honey bucket after all.

Year 8: Moving to Quinhagak

Quinhagak, the biggest village we taught in.

Quinhagak was the largest village we taught in. It is situated on the Kanektok river, near the Arolik river, approximately a mile from the Kuskokwim Bay of the Bering Sea. The Yup'ik name for the village is Kuinerraq, meaning "new river channel." It had solid ground with lots of gravel. The coast was nothing like the Oregon Coast. There were mud flats as far as you could see and no white, sandy beaches. It was about a 20-minute walk through weeds from our village to the coast.

Ken Groves was the school principal. Ken and his wife Peggy were great. They had lived and taught in Malaysia and shared some of their adventures with me. I dreamed that maybe this would be the island we might live on some day. Ken and Peggy were an adorable couple and fun to work with. Ken was easygoing and did a wonderful job as principal, keeping the villagers, students, and staff connected and happy. Peggy was also a great teacher and a good friend. She was cute, talented, and petite. A good wind could blow her away, and almost did a time or two.

Another teacher, Suzanne, taught English as a second language and a number of other subjects. No one taught only one subject in the village schools. She is a beautiful energetic person, very intelligent with the most compassionate nature of anyone I know. Suzanne had a number of health problems, but to look at her you would never have guessed what she had been through in her short life time. She knew several languages and had taught English as a second language in a couple of different countries. She had never married or had children, but she treated her students like they were her own. I would never have been brave enough to go off on an adventure like this by myself.

What more can I say about Suzanne? She became my best friend and I love her. Almost every day Suzanne and I walked either to the coast and back or up and down the gravel road that led through the village to the airstrip. This was our exercise time, walking and talking; usually there would be several dogs following along with us.

We became friends with Fuzzy and his wife Carol who operated an airplane service and lived close to the airstrip in Quinhagak. At one time they had a sports flying business in Minnesota. Fuzzy was an excellent pilot and I felt safe flying with him most of the time. It was really nice to have a plane at your disposal right in the village. He would often bring fresh fruits and vegetables back from Bethel on his trips home.

Flying in the bush was always scary. There were times when you couldn't see anything. They called it a whiteout and it was like flying in a milk bottle. Pilots can easily get disoriented and fly upside down without knowing it. Other times the wind would be so strong the ride would be up and down and landing was a challenge. Fuzzy was landing in one of

My dear friend Suzanne at Bob's party.

those wind storms and I think we made three passes, but each time the wind would blow us way off the runway. He would go up again, trying to get down between gusts. Needless to say, my heart was in my mouth and I was silently praying for a safe landing. Fuzzy never seemed anxious, or at least he never showed it, calmly whistling the tune they play at the horse races when the horses come out. He was a character.

We loved spending time with Fuzzy and Carol. They were both warm and welcoming. We enjoyed many "happy hours" at their house. One time Bob helped Fuzzy move some barrels and afterward they had a few drinks. After that, whenever they had a few drinks together and I wondered where they were, it was referred to as they were "moving barrels."

Tina and Ken Ferringer, two more teachers at the school, lived across the road from Suzanne. They lived in similar housing that had been newly built by the school district. They had two young boys. As were most of the men who came to Alaska, Ken was an outdoorsman like Bob and they had a trap line together and trapped red fox and rabbits. Bob did a lot of trapping. He trapped and skinned the red fox. They were beautiful hides.

For me it was always a worry that he would cut himself and get

rabies. The fox and some dogs were known to have rabies in the area. Occasionally, we saw a fox on our walks in the village. I always turned back when I saw one for fear they would be sick and come after me. I know I spent a lot of time worrying

The men posing with their red fox hides.

about things that never happened. My mother always said I was born scared. Even a few days old I would grasp on to her sleeve or collar afraid she would drop me.

Life in Quinhagak

The school secretary Diana, was a warm young *gussock* woman who was married to a native. Not being able to have children of their own, they adopted a boy and girl, both from relatives in the village. Diana was a hard worker and an excellent mother, living the village life much as the other Eskimo women did. Her parents lived in Ashland, Oregon and we did get to meet them one summer while we were visiting in Ashland. A few years after we left the village we received the sad news that Diana had been shot by her adopted teenage son. Apparently it was not accidental.

The summer before we moved to Quinhagak there was an incident in the village where several of the teenagers got into the school, stole some duplicating fluid, and mixed it with punch. Those who drank it became ill and had to be transported to the hospital. Not all survived without permanent damage. One girl who had to be revived several times during the flight to the hospital had brain damage. I didn't know any of the teenagers before the incident, but you could tell from their learning and behavior problems which students had been involved in the party.

This beautiful 16-year-old girl who stopped breathing on the way to the hospital had short-term memory loss and anger problems. She often became frustrated and walked out of class. Sometimes she would be verbally abusive and destructive. She was in one of my classes. At first I thought I couldn't work with her, but with patience and a lot of time, she became one of my favorites.

Drugs, intermarriages, poor health care, and accidents all were contributing factors for many of the behavioral problems in the children. A full time special education teacher was provided in every school to accommodate the large number of learning disabilities.

Our living conditions were greatly improved in Quinhagak. We lived in the old BIA teacher housing, which had running water. The bathroom had a shower and sink, but we still had a honey bucket, the bane of my existence. There was a laundry room with a washer and dryer, and a regular kitchen with electric range and refrigerator. The bedroom had a full-sized bed, a dresser, and even a closet. The living room had real furniture. We had a front and back door that locked. Our house was about a quarter of a mile from the school. Ken and Peggy lived in an apartment in the BIA school across the road from our house. At the end of the street there were three teacher houses similar to the ones we had lived in while in Atmautluak. There was a gravel road from one end of the village to the airstrip.

Quinhagak Infrastructure

Quinhagak had a store where you could buy canned goods, some clothing, and hardware. Occasionally, they had fresh vegetables and ice cream. Almost everyone had a three wheeler and snow machine. Many of the families owned boats. The main income was from fishing in the summers. The Kuskokwim river is 702 miles long and a great fishing hole. Subsistence fishing villages once relied on Chinook salmon which were plentiful at one time, now the subsistence fishermen on the Lower River are hauling in whitefish, chums, sockeyes, and only the occasional Chinook.

Because Quinahagak was the starting point for a sport fishing trip along the Kuskokwim River and its tributaries operated by Kuskokwim Wilderness Adventues, Fuzzy provided flight service to many of these fishermen. Groups from large cities in Alaska, the lower 48, other villages, and even from other countries, such as Russia often flew to Quinhagak for a sport camping and fishing adventure along the river.

Fuzzy had flown a group of Russians to Quinahagak who had reservations on a chartered fishing trip up the river. On guided trips they'd camp for weeks along the river. This group stayed with Fuzzy and his wife Carol one night before leaving, so we got to meet them and have dinner together. Fuzzy had a phone in the shape of a tennis shoe. One Russian woman was so amused by that phone. She kept picking it up and pretending she was the investigator from the television show "Get Smart." Most knew enough English to communicate.

We bought new luggage in the summer before we traveled to Quinhagak, and although we had our name on all our suitcases, I took one from the airport in Bethel that looked like ours and didn't notice that it belonged to someone else until we were walking down the road to our house. Bob was carrying two of our suitcases and I was walking behind him carrying some smaller luggage. I could tell the two suitcases didn't match. When we looked at the tags one belonged to a traveler in Bethel. We immediately contacted the airport and sent the wrong suitcase back on the next flight.

It took several days for us to get our suitcase delivered to us. That particular piece of luggage had all Bob's fishing gear in it, but it didn't slow him down. To show how easy it was to catch salmon in that river, Bob cut out the red section of a coke can, tied it to a hook, and soon even I was catching huge salmon. I learned many ways to prepare salmon and actually got to the point where I didn't want to eat salmon any more.

We still had the dreaded honey buckets, but this village had a different system for disposing of the waste. They had metal containers with lids much like a small trailer. They were shaped larger at the top than at the bottom. These were placed between every two or three houses like our garbage cans. We would empty our honey buckets into the large container and every week the maintenance man would hook it up to his three wheeler and haul it away to be dumped into a pond at the end of the village. We called it honey-bucket lake. In the winter when the contents froze, it was easier to dump them because of the shape. These frozen bricks thawed in the spring and you can imagine the smell. Fuzzy often joked about selling some prime real estate around the lake.

Cat Stories

As in the other two villages we'd lived, the natives here feared cats. One evening I saw a mouse run under the laundry room door. I couldn't see where it went so I was nervous about going to bed that night. Bob was not scared of a little mouse and assured me that it couldn't get up on the bed. Sometime during the night, however, I was awakened by something crawling on my leg. I jumped up, pulled back the covers, but didn't see anything. By then Bob was awake and a little crabby about my fear of a mouse. He said, "There is nothing in the bed. You just had a nightmare because you were thinking about it before you went to sleep." I sort of calmed down and went to the kitchen, got a drink of water, and when I went back and pulled out the blanket, a mouse ran under my pillow. This time I screamed hysterically and ran out to the living room.

I have no explanation as to why a grown woman is so afraid of a tiny mouse, but seeing a mouse scares the #@%# out of me. After a few minutes, Bob brought the dead creature for me to see that it was no longer a threat. I had to change the sheets before I went to sleep. The next summer we brought a black cat back with us to take care of the mouse problem. This cat was wonderful in more ways than catching mice.

Our cat protected us from burglars and mice, but couldn't fight snow drifts.

All the teachers had a meeting for four days in Bethel. While we were gone, most of the teacher houses were broken into by a group of teenagers. They vandalized all the teacher's things, and found alcohol in some homes, which they drank. They cut the cushions on couches, stole jewelry, and Suzanne had bubble bath in what looked like a champaign bottle. Someone drank it. We know this because they were inexperienced vandals. They used a camera in one of the houses to take pictures of themselves doing some of the mischief, including drinking out of the bubble bath bottle and wearing someone's sombrero. Then they forgot to take the camera with the film in it.

Our house escaped any damage. I'm sure it was because this black cat sat in the window and they didn't chance it. The cat was more afraid of them, but they didn't know that. Whenever anyone came to the house the cat would hide. The students were identified from the pictures and given a slap on the wrist. I couldn't believe it, but the teachers took the brunt of the blame. Because it was a dry village they were not supposed to have alcohol in their homes.

During a snowstorm our black cat was under the house by the warm heat pipes and wouldn't come out. We could hear him meowing and dug the snow away from the entrance leading under the house, but he still wouldn't come out. It was several days before we got someone to go under there and actually carry him out.

During our daily walks Suzanne and I tried to cure the world's problems. Suzanne loved dogs and her dog "Kit" was always with her, along with any dog that was loose in the village. One beautiful malamute we called "Toom," usually followed us. She had a large tumor on her back and no one seemed to claim her. Suzanne had such a big heart and it hurt her to see a chained up dog in pain. Another time we came across a sled dog that was tied with a rope around his neck. It was so tight it had rubbed the poor dog's neck raw and was bleeding. Suzanne got a new collar and salve and doctored the injured dog until it healed. She wasn't afraid of chained dogs. I felt sorry for them, but not brave enough to go try to help them.

Crafts

One day while we were walking on the beach we saw a dead whale. Wondering if the whale had ivory teeth, we looked inside the whale's

Some of the whale teeth with the scrimshaw and hardware added.

mouth. They were ivory, but not loose enough for us to pull. We waited for several weeks, checking every few days to see if the whale had rotted enough to let us pull the teeth. The rotting fish smell was horrendous. We wore scarves over our mouths and nose and wore gloves.

With pliers and knives we managed to pull a few of the teeth. Eventually, after many trips to the coast we were able to pull all the beluga whale's teeth.

When we returned with our treasures, Bob was reluctant to let us in the house. He said we stunk. We washed our treasures and soaked them in a jar of Clorox. After much scrubbing and sanding we had beautiful ivory teeth. Paul, a village native, created amazing scrimshaw, making them into priceless keepsakes for us to share with our friends and family.

Many of the natives were talented artists. Paul taught scrimshaw and ivory carving at the school. With his help, I made two ivory rings and I bought an ivory bracelet for my sister Tillie. She loved bracelets and wore it so much it had to be restrung. Bob also made some ivory jewelry and bought me an ivory bracelet that Paul had scrimshawed native scenes on each ivory square.

The women made Eskimo dolls, wove gorgeous baskets, and made mukluks, and beaver and otter hats. They also made decorations, jewelry, and yo-yos. They dried the grass for the baskets, made the dye, and had the patience to weave baskets that took many hours to make.

An authentic native basket with lid along with my painstaking effort (sitting upside down).

Unless you made one you could not imagine how much work and love went into one of their creations. I worked six weeks on one small basket that would have taken an Eskimo woman a few hours to make and it would have looked much better than the one I made. However, I was proud of my accomplishment, and it made me understand why they could get so much money for their art.

A Federal program provided natives financial assistance to get their college degrees and become teachers. This was a great incentive for a couple of the young people in the village to become teachers and come back and teach in their village. Along with this program came the proposed change in teaching the first four grades in their native language, Yup'ik. It was felt that children learn faster if they are taught in their native language. All the teachers were required to take a course in Yup'ik.

The biggest problem I saw with this program was that Yup'ik was never a written language. It was only oral. They were teaching the children to read and write in a language that had no books or newspapers. Teaching them colors and numbers in Yup'ik and then in third and fourth grade

Some native dolls.

converting this material into English totally confused me. However, the native teachers were hired to teach the primary grades. For the young people to get a college degree and come back and improve the lives of their families was wonderful. It is always good to preserve native culture, and I hope the program was successful.

One afternoon an Eskimo man that I didn't know, but had heard disturbing stories about, knocked on my door. He was selling some jewelry he made. Actually it was very ugly. It reminded me of something a witch doctor would wear. It had little pointed pieces of ivory marked with a black dot between colored beads. I was afraid of him and what he would do, so to get him to leave I bought this $40 "craft" necklace from him. I sent it to my mom and she wasn't impressed. Some years later I saw it at a garage sale.

In one family's home I observed a bowl on their kitchen table that looked much like a goldfish bowl, except there were small black fish swimming in it. Thinking they were pets, I asked about the fish. I was aghast when the Eskimo man scooped one of the fish out of the bowl and ate it raw and alive! I later found out these fish, known as Blackfish, were their version of sushi. Blackfish can withstand partial freezing. They only reside in Alaska and Siberia and have the unique ability of being able to breathe air. Blackfish can survive in stagnant tundra pools nearly devoid of oxygen and even in moist tundra mosses for extended periods.

School

Bob's classroom in Quinahagak was amazing. He had some live animals. Someone found a bat in the local store. Probably came in with some produce. No one had ever seen a bat in the village. Bob kept it in a glass cage and the children, adults, and even the grandparents came to see the bat. I'm not sure why the bat died, but he lasted until after Halloween. A vampire bat? Maybe.

One of Bob's students found an injured baby owl and brought it to class. Bob had to amputate one wing, so the owl would never be able to fly. I fell in love with the tiny critter and wanted to take it to a vet if he survived the trauma of his injuries. Bob crushed some penicillin pills and gave it to him with water. When he was on the mend, Bob put a live mouse in the cage and when he ate it, his chance of survival improved. I don't know how long he survived, but he remained the school pet for some time.

Bob also had an incubator and he hatched some quail eggs. The students observed them hatch, grow up, and produce eggs and raise more birds. The adult quail were mean to each other and had to be separated. Snakes and spiders were not my favorite, but they were all tenants in Bob's classroom.

The gym was the social gathering place for the village. Besides the sporting events, we organized after-school activities to keep the kids busy. We had sock hops, Saturday night dances, carnivals, and the biggest occasion for the teenagers was the annual prom. It took weeks of planning, ordering, and decorating the gym for this special night. The whole high school took part. The seniors were the ones who decided on a theme and it went from there.

I think the whole month before the prom was busy every day after school and weekends making preparations. The gym looked amazing. The kids ordered long stemmed glasses and we had special fancy drinks (nonalcoholic). We had party food, a DJ, someone taking pictures of each couple as they came in, beautiful decorations, plus a strobe light, dressed up boys and girls with happy faces and expectations of a Cinderella ball. The King and Queen were crowned and the kids danced until midnight. The cleanup was supervised by the staff the next day. Seemed like there was always something to do.

Village Life

Bob had tried to quit smoking again and I hid the cigarettes that he had left in the house so he wouldn't be tempted. I noticed that sometimes the cigarettes were missing and blamed Bob for finding them. I had my ivory whale's teeth and a $100 bill hidden in a pocket of a suitcase I was taking home for the summer. This suitcase was covered by a blanket at the bottom of my closet. On Easter we were all having dinner at Ken and Peggy's house and I went to get my scrimshawed whales teeth to show everyone. The teeth were still there, but the $100 bill was gone. The cigarettes were also missing.

I'm not sure if anything else was stolen, but someone had to have gone through all the drawers and pockets to find these things. Who goes through your suitcase pockets? Anyway we were sure to lock our doors whenever we left after that.

I got a lot of reading done while in the villages. There was not much worth watching on TV, although it was better than at our first village. I watched a couple of soaps, "All My Children" and "General Hospital" which were on during the day. We even had a phone in our house.

Debbie was hired to teach in the village for a couple years. She was a single mom and had the sweetest little boy about the same age as one of my grandsons. In fact, he could have fit right in my family with his big blue eyes and blonde hair. We bonded and little Cary spent many afternoons playing at my house. The first thing he did when he got there was take off his shoes and socks. Usually they would be wet and I had a dryer. We had this one thing in common, we liked to go barefoot. We kept in touch for several years after we left Alaska. I enjoyed the school pictures he sent me.

It was always time for a party or some kind of gathering with the teachers. We celebrated birthdays, holidays, anniversaries, or if nothing was happening that week, we would make up a holiday. We shared our letters and treats from home and played every card and board game available.

My Classes

Teaching in Quinhagak was more like my experiences teaching in Akiak. I had a couple classes. I taught keyboarding on the computers to junior high and high school students. I learned many things along with the students, including how to cut and paste, and how to make banners and posters. I taught home economics and a craft class. These were all elective classes. I had a mixture of boys and girls, which was fun. In the craft class we made stuffed animals. Some were from kits and some were from things that they had in their homes. They made snakes out of neckties, and soft picture frames, soft boxes, and some soft baskets. The picture frames, boxes and baskets were made from cloth, batting, and a lot of glue and hand sewing. They were easy and fun for the kids to make and usually turned out looking good, which made the students proud of their finished products. We also did some tie-dye and fabric painting. They designed their own T-shirts and sweatshirts.

My brother-in-law owned a ceramic business in Oregon and he sent me greenware, paints, brushes, everything I needed to teach the kids how to paint ceramics. We also had members of the community come in and work with the kids on ivory carving, skin sewing, and basketmaking.

Like in Akiak, we had a bakery in Quinhagak. It was so much fun and the villagers loved it. Because we had more students in the class we were able to have a larger bakery. We did a unit on family living that I felt would be helpful to these teenagers. Topics included how to balance a checkbook, how to write checks, make a budget, interview for a job, phone techniques, and child care. They actually cared for a sack of sugar as if it were a baby for a week. Not many of the sacks of sugar survived the whole week. One was left in a locker for the weekend; one was opened and used to bake a cake. Most were not ready to be tied down to a baby and left them with their moms or grandmothers.

I also worked in the library cataloguing the books and arranging them on the shelves. Quinhagak had a fabulous library and a librarian. I had the opportunity to fill in for her sometimes. I enjoyed helping the kids pick out a book to read and returning the books they had read. They also had a study hall in the library where I helped students research material for essays.

Village life

Like all small towns, there was a lot of gossip and rumors in Quin-hagak. One single mom was involved with a man that abused her frequently. After a beating she would have him arrested, but shortly after his release she would take him back. There was talk of their getting married. I'm not certain that ever happened. Her 12-year-old daughter frequently climbed out her window and spent the night at her cousin's house when the boyfriend was visiting. She told her cousin that he was molesting her and he'd threatened that if she told anyone he would kill her and whoever she told. These little girls had to deal with this on their own. I don't know if the mother was aware of what was going on, but the little girl couldn't tell her or he might have killed her. Rumor has it that the cousin told her dad and he moved his whole family to another town in Alaska where his children would be safe and away from the drinking and abuse.

Fuzzy's wife Carol was such a nice woman and was friendly to every-one. Annie, a single woman in the village, and Carol became good friends. They spent a lot of time together. Then there were rumors that Fuzzy's walk in the mornings led to Annie's house. Footprints in the snow were incriminating. It doesn't take long for talk to get around in a small village where everyone knows your business. Carol packed up and moved home to Minnesota. I kept in touch with Carol for many years after she left, but eventually lost track of her. I often think about her fondly. She made life in Quinhagak fun and we shared many good times. I once said I liked the sweater she was knitting and she gave it to me. I don't wear it anymore, but have kept it all these years as a reminder of her generosity.

We did a lot of our shopping by catalogue. I found a picture of the sweetest tea set in one of Suzanne's catalogues. It was a replica of Catherine from Russia. I was obsessed with it and kept talking about it. Everyone in the village was aware that I wanted it and my birthday was coming up soon. When we went home for Christmas that year I found the blue and white tea set under the tree from Santa.

One of the customs that was the most fun was the gift toss from the roof. When a boy killed his first wild animal, or reached a certain age, the parent or grandparent would buy a bunch of small items, take them up on the roof, and anyone who wanted to celebrate with them would stand down below. They usually let the older ladies stand in front. Then, they would toss stuff down and if you caught it, it was yours. They were always friendly encounters with lots of laughter.

I heard stories about farting contests, but never was invited to one. I think that was something that was done in the past. I attended a few of their women's events where they played games. They sat cross-legged on the gym floor in a circle. Most of them wore *guspuks* (a long-sleeved blouse with pockets in the front and a high neck. This was to keep the mosquitoes from biting them.) One person went around the circle and tried to make someone laugh. If they laughed they would join the person trying to make people laugh, until the last somber person was left. This person was the winner. They also played some relays. It was always fun and included lots of laughter.

At Christmas, the school staff had a Christmas party with a white elephant gift exchange. I called it a Pirate Game because you could steal from someone. We also played a lot of board games with the other teachers—Pictionary, Trivial Pursuit, rummy tiles, charades, and if we didn't have one of those games handy we played a dictionary game. I still get the giggles when I think about the time we were playing Trivial Pursuit. I read the question: "Which planet is bigger than Uranus? Bob grabbed the card away from me and thought I was being silly and making up the question. Everyone was laughing at that one and I still laugh when I think about it. Cribbage was the main card game while we were there. All the village kids knew how to play and were good at it.

Winter was the most challenging at the coastal village. The wind blew almost every day. The snow was cold and dry and almost impossible to make snowmen or anything other than an ice ball from the heat of your hand. There was not a lot of snow all over the ground because the wind blew it and what was left formed a layer of ice and some snow banks. Some days the wind was so fierce that it was impossible for me to walk to the school. Peggy, who weighed less than a hundred pounds, was literally picked up and blown away. Ken and Bob had to rescue her. Aside from the strong wind, the ground was a sheet of ice. Walking on that was impossible.

One afternoon after school, Suzanne had a pair of clamp-ons (devices that clamp onto your shoes and have spikes on the bottom to poke into the ice to keep you from slipping) that she said she would share with me. We each put one on our outside foot, held on to each other, and tried to maneuver the half mile to our houses. We looked like the two stooges. The wind blew us around in a circle and we ended up laughing so hard we were crying. Seeing our predicament, a fellow driving by in a pickup stopped and gave us a ride to the end of the road. Suzanne's house was at the end of the road, but mine was up a little incline farther off the road. To reach my house I had to crawl on my hands and knees, grabbing for any vegetation that would give me a little boost.

I always wore a scarf and wrapped it around my face with only my eyes showing. Some people wore ski masks. Uncovered skin would freeze in seconds. I had icicles on my eyes and nose. Nothing is more attractive than frozen snot that gets stuck on your scarf. It was so cold on those windy days when I walked to the school for my afternoon classes that I wondered how long it would take for someone to find me if I passed out on the road. The cold wind literally took my breath away. One of the blizzards covered the front of our house. You could walk right up on the roof. That was the only time the snow was wet enough to build a snowman. Good thing we had a back door so we could escape.

During the third year in Quinhagak, Bob caught a cold in the winter and couldn't shake it. By spring of 1990, he was complaining about being extremely tired and had a small lump on his neck. He was no longer able to walk his trap line and rode his ATV everywhere. That spring when we landed in Portland, my sister Tillie and her husband Ken, picked us up at the airport. We spent the rest of the day and night with them before we rented a car and drove home to Eugene.

Bob borrowed Tillie and Ken's car to visit his sisters while we were in the Portland area. His sister Lois gave him a box of trick candy. It looked exactly like a box of Whitman's chocolates, but they were plastic and stuck to the bottom of the box. After dinner he gave Tillie the box of candy and we all had a good laugh. The funny thing about that box of candy was that it went around for years and somehow ended up at my brother John's house. He was having a garage sale and put a 50 cent tag on it. Lois, who started the whole thing, saw that box of candy at the sale and said, "I had one like this a few years ago and had so much fun with it." She bought it and then we told her it was the exact same one she had before.

As soon as we were home in Springfield we made an appointment for Bob to see his doctor. They didn't waste any time getting him in. In fact, Bob saw the doctor the next day. After an examination, blood work, and an x-ray, the doctor called and asked Bob to come in the next morning. The diagnosis was chronic lymphocytic leukemia. Needless to say, it was not what we had hoped to hear and we were devastated. But that didn't last long; Bob didn't complain or brood about "why me." He went on and lived every day to the fullest. He had never had a brand new car so we went out and bought him a 1990 Thunderbird Super Coupe.

That year while he was in treatment he remodeled the upstairs of our house. He took the year off as sick leave and between working on the house when he felt well enough he went fishing. My son Aaron, Stephanie, and their baby girl Danielle Brianna were living in our house with us. Dani was Papa's helper and when he took a nap so did Dani. Stephanie was an angel. They had planned to live in our house while we were in Alaska to allow them to save enough to make a down payment on a house of their own. When Bob got sick, we all ended up living together. She never complained although I know it was hard to share a house with your in-laws when you are newly married and have a baby. Bob and I both loved having them there and being able to bond with little Dani. When the baby would cry in the mornings, Stephanie put her in her carrier and walked around outside so they wouldn't wake Papa Bob.

During this time, my mother was battling Alzheimer's and would sometimes stay a few days with us. She loved the baby, Danielle and would get up in the night and pick her up out of her crib, so we all had to be watchful of her. Our house was not that big, but always overflowing during the summer, and this year there was Jeff and his son Josh, and Jason, who would be home from college, and Mindy and her family, who stayed with Her husband's parents, Mac and Marian, but spent a lot of time with us.

That fall, Bob and I took a trip to Mexico along with Bob's older brother Selmer. Bob's brother Lynn and his wife Deloris had built a 70-foot cement bottom sailboat called "Endless Summer" that they lived in and sailed from a port in Escondido, Mexico. We spent a couple weeks sailing, fishing, and collecting shells with a new beach view every morning. Except for one trip to La Paz during a storm, sailing was amazing. On that trip Lynn was delivering a boat to La Paz for repair and we went along. It was such a scary trip. I white-knuckled it the whole way. The sea was tipping and turning the boat and I was sure it was going to flip over. We had to anchor for the night and I don't think I slept a wink. I couldn't go in the cabin for fear of sea sickness. I just kept looking at the horizon.

While we were in La Paz it was fun. The trip back was not as scary until we ran into darkness. I don't know how Lynn managed to get that boat back just by the light of the moon. We had lobster for Thanksgiving dinner and slept on the deck some nights under the stars. Every day at sundown we had happy hour. These tropical places were quite a contrast to the past years we had spent in Alaska.

Our son Jason with Bob in Quinhagak.

Between treatments, we took a trip to Mexico with my brother John and his wife Linda. Bob didn't let on if he was not feeling well. He was amazing through it all. By spring he was feeling better and the lymph nodes were no longer swollen. His doctor said he could go back to his teaching job. If he noticed any symptoms he should come home for further treatment.

That August our son Jason went with us to the village. All our children were supportive and helpful during Bob's illness. Jason was single and we probably leaned on him more than we should have. Jason could make a trip to the doctor fun. He was such good medicine for his dad and me. He stayed with us in the village until he thought his dad was doing okay. The village girls all loved Jason and he got a first-hand view of village life. He learned how to make dry fish and had the opportunity to taste all the different native cuisine, plus do some salmon fishing.

On October 9th we were blessed with another grandson. October 9th was also Bob's birthday, his oldest grandson Joshua's birthday, Joshua's mother's birthday, and now his youngest grandson's birthday. Aaron was the third son after Jeff and Jason and when his dad called him it usually came out J… aren. Aaron said at one time, "If I have a little boy I am going to call him Jaren so someone will answer when my dad calls." Well, he got his baby boy, but he named him, Robert, after his father. Later that month, Bob developed some enlarged lymph nodes. Because there was no available medical care for him in the village, we had to pack up and go home. This time for good.

Bob's farewell party.

We held a mini-garage sale and sold or gave away all our household things: the three wheeler, snow machine, boat, etc. The school gave us a bittersweet going away party. All the kids signed a big stuffed parrot for Bob and I got a fat rabbit. It was hard saying goodbye to the students and many new friends we had made in Alaska, but we were going home to be with our family and friends in Oregon.

Final Departure

As we boarded the plane and flew out of Alaska for the last time, I looked down at the frozen tundra and the village. I thought, even though it had sometimes been difficult, I wouldn't trade the experiences and the friends we made for anything.

Alaska was good for us. I had a hard time adjusting to the culture and all the inconvenience and cold weather, but I have so many happy memories of the years we spent with these wonderful people. The natives, and the teachers who came to live there taught me so much about life and survival. Living in the bush was harsh. The weather could be as cold as 90 degrees below zero with wind chill.

Aside from the miserable weather there was poor health care, too many accidental drownings, and alcohol related deaths. The native women were resourceful and hard working in a harsh country. They did the cooking, cleaning, bore the children and cared for them and their grandchildren, tanned hides and did skin sewing, gathered reeds and made baskets, some fished through the ice, picked berries, entertained, cleaned, and preserved the fish and game the husband brought home, and some put up with a drunken husband. Alaska was still a man's country and I had actually survived a "nine-month" camping trip that lasted 12 years.

After We Came Home

Bob took one more trip on his brother's boat with several of his brothers and sisters. It was good for them to spend some time together and reminisce. One of his sisters said, "I fell in love with my brother all over again." The next few years were spent fixing up our old house, traveling, spending time with our children and grandchildren, and visiting with old friends. Bob loved working with wood and in his spare time he made beautiful myrtlewood bowls, vases, boxes, and furniture. He sold some at the Made in Oregon craft store and we went to several bazaars.

He made many beautiful pieces of furniture, a four-poster bed frame, a cedar chest, a hall tree with mirror, a mini hutch, a cabinet for a tea set, a treasure chest, plant stands, two rocking chairs for his grandchildren, etc. He left a shop full of wood and machines. Some of the myrtle wood was given to him by a friend, Jack Morgan. Jack lived in Coos Bay and spent most of his life as a commercial fisherman. Bob and Jack became friends while Bob was commercial fishing on his boat the Phyllis.

The first year we were in Alaska our son Jeff and his friend Joel tried their hand at fishing. Something always went wrong and they had to be towed in by the Coast Guard. After the third time, the Coast Guard told them to please stay off of the ocean. It probably was a good idea. The boat had some issues and they were not prepared to deal with them.

Although sick, Bob was still passionate about nature and being outdoors. We bought a motorhome so we could go camping and fishing. That motorhome was an albatross, but it did allow him to do some camping. We took one trip to Lamola Lake in Southern Oregon, where Jason worked for the Forest Service. And we spent some time at Crater Lake. Our first adventure in our motorhome was for a week at Dorena Lake in Cottage Grove, then several times to the Oregon Coast.

One trip to the Oregon Coast went well until on our way home, the motorhome died a few miles out of Reedsport right by a curve and next to a guardrail. Bob couldn't even get out the door. I squeezed out and luckily a man stopped with a cell phone and called a tow truck for us. We spent several hours at the service station while they tried to find out what was wrong. The second gas tank had a block in the line and when Bob switched gas tanks it stopped working although the second tank was full. All we needed was to put gas in the empty tank and we were on our way again. Bob wasn't feeling well that day but drove home. I was afraid to drive that monstrosity, but might have given it a try if I absolutely had to.

Despite his many health problems, Bob never complained. He worked in the yard, planted a garden every year, and went out to make cord wood or gather a supply of walnut or cedar for woodworking projects. He bought a whole truckload of myrtle wood board months before he died. He never stopped living. He did more than he probably should have. He once said that after a hard day's work it always made him feel good. Somehow after a hard day's work now he didn't have the same result.

At one point, Bob needed a port put into his chest to get treatments. This had to be flushed every day in a sterile environment. When he came home from the hospital a nurse came out every day for a week to teach me how to do it. It is amazing what you can do if you have to. I would never have thought it was possible for me to actually do some of the things I had to do. It became my morning ritual.

I would get the packet of supplies, wash my hands, close the bedroom door so no one or any animal would be there, put on a mask and open the sterile package. After I flushed the tubing I would clean the area and put on another bandage. Because I was so nervous treating him it took me at least a half hour to do this job the nurse did in 10 minutes.

Bob had chemotherapy, radiation, blood transfusions, and a procedure where they took his blood out and filtered out some of the many white blood cells. This was done in the dialysis part of the hospital. Even when he was in the hospital he was positive and telling his funny, or not so funny jokes, over and over. "Did you hear about the guy who wanted to be a boxer"? Or, "I can't wait till tomorrow . . ."

He had a theory that as long as he didn't finish things, he would have to live long enough to finish them. He started many times to write a book about the rat farm, the piece of land that he grew up on in Redland. He made gallons of wine that final year, hoping he would live long enough to drink it, and he tried to teach me all the things I would have to do without him, like pruning the fruit trees and roses, and mowing the lawn.

Bob didn't live long enough to take me to our tropical island. He passed away on August 31, 1996. Actually, the island dream was not important anymore. As long as I had the love of my life, it didn't really matter where we lived.

Epilogue

The benefits from the School District were invaluable. Bob was on disability for more than a year, then retired with full medical insurance and a paid-up life insurance policy. I am still on his medical insurance.

We made lifelong friends. Many of them I am still in contact with. Robert and Billie Day retired from their Alaskan adventure and moved back to Idaho. Shortly after their return, they both had health problems and downsized their living situation. Eventually they moved to Oregon in a small retirement community in Woodburn. It was such a blessing to have these dear friends close by. All four of my children found ways to stop by and see the Days whenever they went by Woodburn, and Robert and Billie made it down to many of our family events in Springfield.

They were one of the best things that came out of our time in Alaska. They were a great support for me during Bob's illness. Billie passed away in August 2011, and Robert followed three years later. We always had so much fun together in Alaska and after they moved to Oregon.

Jerry and Helen Keller usually spend some time during their summer in the Lower 48 and stop for a visit and catch me up on what is happening in Bethel and the people from the village. Their children are grown, married, and have given them many grandchildren.

Suzanne retired from Alaska, sold her home in Canada, and moved to Squim, Washington. We keep in touch regularly. She continues to have health problems, but what an angel. My sister Patty and I visited with her last spring, and although she was not feeling well she was such a gracious hostess and we had the best time. She has a beautiful home that she designed and has many friends and a faithful dog named Spiri. We keep in touch often through phone calls and email.

Bill and Debbie have three grown children, are retired and live in Minnesota near their grandchildren. We communicated often up until the last couple years. Twin sister, Kathy Brown, never married but has an adopted child.

Cliff got married and moved to Kaiser, Oregon. We met for coffee a few years ago when he was in Eugene. Terry and Olinka stayed in Alaska. Jim married a native woman Alice, who had a small child, and he also stayed in Alaska.

Carlton and Lucy moved their family to Homer, Alaska for several years. They are now back in Bethel. We usually exchange Christmas cards. I enjoy seeing their family picture every Christmas.

Ken and Peggy retired and moved home to Pensacola, Florida, where they are enjoying the warm weather and more relaxed lifestyle. Peggy was taking tap dancing lessons.

Several of the students I taught in Alaska have found me on Facebook. It is fun to communicate with them now that they are adults with children of their own.

Several years after Bob's death while cleaning out the attic, I came across the beaver hide I'd tanned in Akiak with the patient help of Marian Jackson. She showed me the native skills of scraping, oiling, and stretching the hide over the course of weeks. This was my first attempt at tanning—it turned out beautifully—and it carried so many memories.

Because the "fungus tradition" had ended, I decided to revive the tradition with the beaver pelt. I wrote a letter describing the history of the Bolkan fur and suggested that it should be enjoyed by deserving family members for a year or two and then passed on to another family member, who would enclose a note describing the fur's adventures during its visit with them.

At our 2005 Christmas celebration I gave the fur to my eldest son, Jeff, along with the Bolkan fur's history. It has since passed through the hands of each of my children and is working through the granchildren. The fictional chronicals of its adventures, added by each temporary owner, go with it. The stories are hilarious—who knew a beaver pelt could get in so much trouble?

Jeff, the only one of my children who didn't get to visit us in Alaska remarried a few months before Bob died. He and his wife Sharleen live next door to me, which is a great source of comfort especially now that I am aging. They share four children and five grandchildren. My oldest grandson Joshua graduated from the University of Oregon in journalism. He lives in Portland and writes for and edits several educational magazines. Josh's daughter Ava is 11-years old and my only biological great grandchild.

My daughter Mindy raised her two boys in North Pole, Alaska. After her divorce from Tom she put herself through college and earned her teaching degree. She taught elementary students. Little Brendan got a full scholarship to Duke University and went on to Vanderbilt Law School where he received his law degree and passed the Bar exam. He lives and works in Manhattan, New York. Treg was married in 2013 to Emily and they live and work in Utah. In 2010 Mindy and her new husband David moved back to Oregon.

Jason stayed with me for almost three years after Bob died. He went on a vacation to visit a friend who was working in Japan. Sightseeing in Bali he met Dawn, (a Canadian citizen) who had also lost her father and was traveling with her mother. They met in the hotel lobby and did some sightseeing in Bali together. For the next year they had a long-distance relationship, Jason lived on the west coast in Oregon and Dawn was from Toronto, Canada. They ended up getting married and currently reside in Toronto. They also have a fantastic little girl, Samantha.

Aaron and Stephanie still live in Springfield, Oregon and continue to be always there for me. Their first daughter, Danielle Brianna (Papa called her Princess Brianna) is as sweet as she is beautiful. She works as a doctor's assistant at River Bend Hospital. Little Robert (named after his Papa) joined the Marines out of high school, finished his four years of duty, took classes in Jacksonville, Florida, and is now back in the Springfield area. He recently bought a house in Eugene and is attending the University of Oregon. Baby Hannah grew up to be an amazing young woman. She graduated from Oregon State University and now works in the medical field.

I have been blessed with this beautiful loving family. They are all so special and everyone has the "sweet" gene.

ALSO FROM GLADEYE PRESS

Available for purchase at:

www.gladeyepress.com
Book stores
Amazon

10 Takes: Pacific Northwest Writers Perspectives on Writing
Jennifer Roland
From novelists to poets to playwrights, Jennifer Roland interviews a variety of authors who have one thing in common—they have all chosen to make the Pacific Northwest their home.

Washington's Festivals, Fairs & Celebrations
Janaya Watne
Northwest native and fierce outdoorswoman, Janaya Watne has written an information-packed exploration of Washington's vibrant festival calendar. Tourists as well as the well-established who are looking to find the perfect week, weekend, or one-day trip will enjoy this handy guide.

Oregon's Festivals, Faires & Celebrations
J.V. Bolkan & Sharleen Nelson
From truffles & brews to mosquito fests & digeridoo, in Oregon there's always something to do! This handy travel and event guide includes more than 90 listings—everything from craft brew & wine fests, food- and flower-based celebrations, and music/film festivals to family focused events.

COMING SPRING 2018
from *GLADEYE PRESS FICTION*

The Time Tourists, A Novel
Sharleen Nelson
DANGER. ROMANCE. TIME TRAVEL . . .
Step into time with Imogen Oliver in this first book in the
Dead Relatives, Inc. series as she investigates a young girl
who ran away from home with her boyfriend in 1967 and
never returned, and then travels back to the turn of the
20th century to locate a set of missing stereoscopic glass
plates with a mysterious connection to her own life.

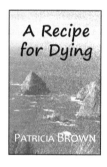

A Recipe for Dying
Patricia Brown
The sleepy seaside town of Sand Beach has a problem.
Older folk are dying, seemingly peacefully, but is it really
the work of a serial killer? Eleanor, a retired teacher,
stumbles into the mystery. With the help of an eclectic
cast of friends she sets out to discover who and what is
ending so many lives.

- Visit www.gladeyepress.com for fantastic deals on these and other
  GladEye Press titles.
- Follow us on Facebook: https://www.facebook.com/GladEyePress/
- All GladEye titles can be ordered from your local book store and
  Amazon.com.

CPSIA information can be obtained
at www.ICGtesting.com
Printed in the USA
FSHW04n1510220318
45793FS

9 780991 193172